TRUST NO ONE
Cybersecurity Basics for Home and Business

Using Sun Tzu and modern military intelligence strategies to implement a cybersecurity mindset in any organization

By Samuel D. Bass

ISBN: 978-0-9898853-9-3

Please review this book. All constructive comments are welcomed and appreciated!

ABOUT THE AUTHOR

Samuel D. Bass, Colonel, USAF (Retired), CISSP®

Sam recently retired after serving 25 years in the US Air Force. He held leadership positions in cyberspace security, information systems operations and management, and nuclear weapon systems operations. During his career, he led large and small teams in various national security positions around the United States to include two assignments to the Pentagon, served in a deployable combat communications unit in Germany, and advised bilateral mission partners in Iraq and Japan. He last served as the Director of Cyberspace Operations, Headquarters 5th Air Force, Tokyo, Japan. He holds master's degrees from the Air Force Institute of Technology, Embry-Riddle Aeronautical University and Air University, and is a Certified Information Systems Security Professional.

The views expressed are those of the author and do not reflect the official policy or position of the Department of Defense or the U.S. Government.

FOREWORD

Worldwide Cyber War

Today, almost every single man, woman and child in America is actively engaged in cyberspace. Families share photographs and location data with loved ones (and often strangers) in the same town or on the other side of the planet. We live in residences blanketed by wifi networks connected to baby monitors and smart refrigerators. Bits of our personal and financial data is stored electronically around the country. And for most businesses, sharing information via financial networks, email and web pages is absolutely essential. Simply put, nearly all of our sensitive personal and business data is stored on phones, computers, or somewhere in the cloud.

But a cyberwar is raging. Hackers seek money. Developing economies seek technology. Political and business adversaries seek advantage. In cyberspace, all of these are just a few mouse-clicks away.

If groups of thieves and vandals were raiding local grocery stores and bank vaults, police would be deployed. If another country attacked America's finance and industry sectors with armed soldiers, the US military would be called in to action.

But how do we respond to cyber attacks? Attack back? Cut off our connection to the world? We could bolster our defenses, but how can that be completely effective when some attacks are against newly discovered vulnerabilities in hardware or software that haven't been fixed by the vendor?

We could read other books about what some other organization did to protect itself and hope that the model used there will help protect us too. But the attacks continue to evolve from month to month, and the scope and pace is increasing rather than declining. So what can we do?

I wrote this book to instill in you a *cybersecurity mindset*, whether you run a large company or you just started your first job and opened your first bank account. And since cybersecurity affects us all, I wrote this book for readers with little to no knowledge of cybersecurity. My hope is that you will use the ideas in this book to develop a strategic approach to assessing your vulnerabilities and readiness for the war in cyberspace that is already a significant threat to your wealth and privacy.

And most importantly, I wrote this book to be a fast read because you've got a lot of work to secure your cyber assets.

— Samuel D. Bass

Table of Contents

CHAPTER 1

Trust No One?

Cybersecurity For The Rest Of Us

Why should you read this book? There are thousands of books on cybersecurity already available, and many are quite good at painting dire pictures about the state of cybersecurity in homes, businesses, and governments around the world. Some of these books go in to great detail on the additional network security tools and complex processes needed to improve your cybersecurity, and the plans provided in most of these books would help tremendously if followed to the letter. So why do we need another cybersecurity book? Because in my opinion, most of us don't have the expertise to implement these changes or the piles of money needed to hire adequate cybersecurity help. Yet we must quickly come to grips with this seemingly complex and mysterious environment. If you don't think you're already a victim of cybercrime, you either don't know your information has somehow been compromised or it will be soon if you don't quickly embrace some basic cybersecurity principles.

Cyber attackers are becoming increasingly successful at stealing huge repositories of data and fortune. Even as this book was being written in the first quarter of 2018, two major cyber headlines blanketed the news: a vulnerability in the basic design of microprocessors was discovered in January, and most of Atlanta, Georgia's government computers were crippled and held for ransom in March. Both are striking indicators that even more disruptive cyber attacks[1] are in our future.

This book was written to be a quick read for those with little to no experience at all with the cyber environment. It is a cyber book for the rest of us: business executives, small business owners, and professionals of all specialties. If you are in a position to influence the behavior of whatever organization you participate in, you will be able to use this book as a guide for improving security. If you are an executive in a business with a sizable

---

[1] Conduct a web search for either "Atlanta cyber attack" or "Spectre and Meltdown" for more information on these topics.

1

Information Technology (IT) support team, you will be better prepared to support their important security initiatives. If you are a small business owner, you will learn there are things you should be (and in many cases, must be) doing to protect your business. And if you don't have many employees in your small or home business, you alone might be the IT support team and so you must gain a better understanding of the risks in cyber space. The same goes for your family; your devices at home might be putting your business and personal data at risk unless you take some basic cybersecurity precautions.

Regardless of your position or familiarity with cybersecurity, *no one should care more than you* about your sensitive personal and business data.

How To Read This Book

You don't need to know anything about cybersecurity in order to understand this book. You likely have a great deal of experience using a computer or connected device like a smartphone or tablet, so you are probably familiar with basic terms (for example: operating system, patch or update, wifi, Bluetooth, etc.). Interacting with connected devices is a simple fact of modern life, so if you don't know these terms now, you should by the time you finish this book. What you do need is to *be curious.* I've included references in the footnotes and appendices, so if you don't understand something in the book, I encourage you to do a quick web search to become familiar with the topic before continuing. Even if you only have a single connected device, you can't afford not to know the basics of cybersecurity now.

Whether you're the president of a global conglomerate or run a small business from your home, you absolutely must start thinking about cybersecurity in all aspects of your operations and the potential vulnerabilities present. The goal of this book is to foster a cybersecurity mindset that will make you think about security every time you see a connected device in your home or office, every time you get an email, and every time you consider installing new software. You should use the lessons in this book to help instill the same cybersecurity mindset in everyone in your organization, whether they are colleagues, employees or family members.

This book begins with a brief introduction of the cyber war raging around the globe. You will learn some of the basics of how the attackers are succeeding at exploiting the weakest links in our defenses. Since this seems like warfare, we will look to historical advice from the famous

Chinese strategist Sun Tzu. From there, we will quickly review how the US military collects and processes intelligence to support its mission. Finally, we'll explore a cybersecurity process that organizations large and small can tailor to focus their attention on cybersecurity priorities. Rather than re-stating what other books and web sites already provide in painstaking detail, this one simple process will help you concentrate on protecting the systems and data that matter the most to you.

To demonstrate how this process might help businesses, there a few exercises that ask you to conduct some assessments and define cybersecurity objectives for your organization. Do yourself a favor and go through these steps as they will build upon one another and help you establish some important cybersecurity habits. By following these exercises and trying this process in your own organization, this book will help you understand the fact that none of us should ever let our guard down when it comes to cybersecurity. As you use this process to implement some cybersecurity basics in your home or office network, the process will remain a helpful guide for continuous education and more improvements that you may have considered too challenging.

So let's begin. Be curious, be suspicious, and **Trust No One**.

CHAPTER 2
Cyber War

Worst Case Scenario

Consider the smartphone in your pocket and the computers in your home or office. Imagine if you suddenly couldn't get to the data on those devices. You can't see any phone numbers, addresses, or birthday reminders for your friends or colleagues. All of your books, music and movies are unavailable. All of your home videos and photographs: deleted. Those emails or documents about your company's new project have been taken over by someone else. You have no access to your company's research, designs or strategic plans. Somehow, a series of really bad events led to you losing it all. Where would you begin to recover your data? Who would you turn to for help? And how much emotional or financial damage would this cause in your home or business?

It is a scenario that happens all around the world, all the time. And just as there are thousands of stories about cyber breaches in the press, there are countless articles and books that try to provide some insight into the mind of the hacker. But you shouldn't expect that you can simply read some hacking books to quickly learn how to secure your home or office network, particularly without accumulating years of hands-on experience. And we obviously can't be absolutely certain that someone else is protecting our data as many global organizations that have been entrusted with our sensitive information are regularly compromised by hackers. It's a very worrisome situation, but the proverb "worrying is like sitting in a rocking chair; you're doing something, but not going anywhere" applies very well to cybersecurity. So what else can we do besides worrying?

Imagine instead that you knew more about the cyber threats to your data, and that you had taken steps to prepare for this moment. Imagine that you had made backups of your critical data, protected your organization's reputation and brand, and avoided costly legal fees from customer lawsuits.

4

You might have to spend considerable amounts of time and money to restore what was lost, but you wouldn't just be rocking in that chair lamenting about how good things were before it all happened.

Say Goodbye To Hollywood

Around the world, citizens have lived with the very real threat of war. During World War II, Americans on both coasts blacked out their windows at night just in case enemy bombers flew overhead. During the Cold War in the 1960s, students regularly practiced "duck and cover" drills to survive enemy nuclear strikes. Even today, numerous countries around the globe are beset by deadly civil wars. Sadly, entire population groups around the globe have at one time or another prepared for an enemy attack to improve their chances of survival. Yet few of us are even remotely prepared for cyber war.

We all know Hollywood's depiction of cyber war: some brilliant computer programmer driven by a deep-seated desire to destroy the world uses high-powered computers located in a well-hidden bunker to wreak havoc on national banking and power systems. Unfortunately, the reality is much more troubling.

A quick web search for "cyber attack" will generate countless articles about recent large-scale data breaches, wide-spread infections of malicious software, attacks on power and financial systems, and invasions of the privacy of people of all ages. Our personal data is scattered around the Internet, and businesses (some benevolent, others not) are making millions analyzing this data for what we like, where we go, who we know, and where we spend our money. Companies have had intellectual property, electronic records or sensitive communications stolen, usually at significant cost to the organization in terms of lost revenue, lawsuit settlements or loss of market leadership (and in some cases, all three). In the aftermath, the culprits might be identified as powerful state-sponsored hacking teams using advanced cyber weapons. But normally, the hackers are either criminal groups using hacking tools bought on the black market or lone wolves using newly discovered exploits on inexpensive laptops in a cafe. No high-priced supercomputer labs needed, and not just one cyber villain but literally tens of thousands.

But can we honestly call lone wolf attacks a cyber war? There are several definitions for war, ranging from moderate competition between opposing groups to full-on weaponized hostilities. Another definition is that of a sustained campaign against something unwanted, like the "war on drugs" or the "war on poverty."

Certainly the ongoing cyber attacks seen in the news fit somewhere on this spectrum of war. And when your intellectual property is lost, your identity is stolen, or your finances depleted, you certainly feel like it's a personal war. But simply saying we are in a cyber war won't change anything. It's time to not only acknowledge that we are in a global cyber war, but it's time for everyone to prepare for this war.

Sun Tzu's <u>The Art of War</u>

Businesses and governments around the world have been connected to the Internet for several decades now, so many organizations have been bolstering their cyber defenses ever since the first hackers started having fun by defacing web pages. To the Pentagon however, having official web pages defaced by hackers is no laughing matter. Nor is any malicious activity that might have a negative impact on the Department of Defense's ability to protect and defend American citizens at home or abroad. As you can imagine, the Pentagon has placed a high priority on cyber defense and continues to bolster its cybersecurity technologies and capabilities.[2]

When US military members study warfare, they usually begin with Sun Tzu. Even though Sun Tzu was a Chinese general more than 2,500 years ago, his writings on military strategy are still taught today at all levels of American professional military education. His lessons on military intelligence, training, and the chain of command remain relevant in modern armed conflict. Some of Sun Tzu's lessons are also relevant to diplomacy, public administration, and planning, earning his book a large following in business and politics. For many centuries, leaders from numerous nations and industries have benefitted from Sun Tzu's works.

Sun Tzu understood that knowledge truly is power. His book describes the importance of knowledge about the adversary, the terrain, and your own army's capabilities. Sun Tzu said that if you know the enemy and know yourself, you will be victorious. If you know yourself, but not the enemy, your chance of losing the battle is equal to your chance of winning. And if you know neither yourself nor the enemy, you will most likely lose every time.[3] While Sun Tzu wrote this in the time of swords, bows and

---

[2] Please see <u>The Department of Defense Cyber Strategy</u>, April 2015. Available at: https://www.defense.gov/Portals/1/features/2015/0415_cyber-strategy/Final_2015_DoD_CYBER_STRATEGY_for_web.pdf

[3] Sun Tzu, <u>The Art of War</u>, III, 18. Available free on line at:

arrows, I propose that these lessons are just as important in the time of cyberspace. If you haven't already read Sun Tzu, it is short enough that you can read it during a lunch break.

While you don't need to be a Sun Tzu expert to understand this book, his lessons reinforce the fact that leaders should be well-versed in all areas that affect the organization's purpose or mission. Certainly cybersecurity affects numerous crucial organizational functions ranging from facilitating basic daily communications to accessing company finances. Yet a common critique of global cybersecurity in business is that the C-suite executives (CEO, COO, CFO, etc.) aren't active enough in establishing and enforcing company-wide cybersecurity policy. The same applies to heads of families and small business owners; everyone relies on cyberspace, yet many of us are hoping that *someone else* is taking care of our cybersecurity needs.

This book won't teach you cyber attack techniques to hone your defensive skills, nor will it provide strategies for offensive cyber operations. There are plenty of other books on hacking, and they can offer important insights into how someone might attack you. But just as learning how someone hot-wired your car won't bring it back to your driveway, learning how to hack won't bring back your lost data or erase the news headlines about your company's latest security blunder. Similarly, there are likely many more hackers in the world than any of us would be able to summon, so trying to retaliate would likely escalate into a quickly untenable (and frankly, un-winnable) situation. The hackers are out there seeking to exploit any vulnerability they can, and thus our focus will be on one of Sun Tzu's key tenets: avoiding a losing battle.

Armchair General

Any book asking you to start thinking like a soldier or a general without the benefit of years of military training and experience is fanciful at best. So rather than asking you to suddenly think like a military strategist or a disciple of Sun Tzu, I ask you to think instead from a new perspective as an outsider to your present organization, like a security consultant or an insurance adjuster. And when you think about cybersecurity, don't just think of the device itself, like "my computer," or "my phone." You should be most concerned about securing your data on these devices, and you should realize that nearly everyone is (or could become) a potential enemy.

Consider that in your current organization—a business or even a home—you are ultimately responsible for the actions of everyone in your organization, just like a commanding general. Don't assume that someone else will understand what's important to you when making decisions, nor should you assume that everyone on your team will always follow the organization's rules. Anyone in your organization can make a mistake or fall victim to an attack or accident. If you are responsible for leading or training others in your organization, part of your leadership and training should definitely include cybersecurity.

The hackers have declared cyber war, and you're the commander.

CHAPTER 3

Know the Enemy

Plenty of Targets

When a damaging cyber crime is reported in the media, the headline normally summarizes either the staggering number of victims or the extensive amount of damage that is caused. You can find stories about cyber attacks stealing millions of customer credit cards, causing millions of dollars in damage, cancelling thousands of flights or leaving thousands of homes without power. There are victims in every segment of society, from governments to individuals of all ages, even children. Some victim companies might only have only supporting parts of their business on line, say for example a movie production studio or power company. Other victim companies may be tech industry behemoths that operate almost exclusively on line. There are undoubtedly countless hacks on smaller businesses that never get reported in the media, but with enough damage a single attack can completely devastate any organization. Regardless of the industry, any company that operates with only a few devices connected to the Internet can be compromised by motivated hackers.

What are the hackers after with these attacks? We could analyze hundreds of hacks and assess the individual motivations behind them, but there are some general themes identified in numerous cybersecurity studies and reports that are available free on line.[4] In the Retail and Financial sectors, the enemy is primarily after money. When attacking government entities, attackers seek technology and information, money, or even just to make an ideological point. And when a manufacturing business is targeted, the enemy wants trade secrets, designs or inventions that might help them compete. Many other businesses outside of these industries are targeted as well for various reasons, sometimes just because a random scan happens to

---

[4] Find links to sample Cyber Threat Reports in Appendix 6.

find a major vulnerability. One common factor is that successful hacks normally negatively affect the organization's mission and inflict serious financial consequences, ranging from customer lawsuits to outright theft of treasure. Invariably, most hacks incur recovery efforts that may require more time, people and money than the organization is capable of providing without external assistance.

While some businesses might try reducing their on-line presence to limit their exposure to outside hackers, there are multiple instances of attacks by insiders. Disgruntled employees have damaged or destroyed infrastructure and erased data in retaliation for some perceived wrong, and financially strapped employees have tried to benefit by selling valuable insider information. According to numerous reports, as many as 15% of reported cybersecurity attacks were conducted or enabled by insiders. The threat to all organizations is real and present, either from the global internet or the cubicle next to you.

Recalling the Hollywood image of the lone brilliant hacker, the sheer volume of successful cyber attacks would indicate there are either thousands of evil geniuses running around or it's not that difficult to hack. Sadly, software bugs and configuration errors are surprisingly common on our networked devices, and hackers need little more than patience to find and exploit these vulnerabilities.

A New Industry

How long will it take before our computers, phones and networks are secure enough where they can never be hacked? My guess is until humans are essentially alleviated from software development and configuration responsibilities, which probably won't happen until sometime around 2050. Before you write that off as crazy, consider the automobile.

In 1769, the French inventor Cugnot built a steam-powered tricycle, which could be considered the first automobile[5]. About 100 years later, German inventor Karl Benz began building cars with internal combustion gasoline engines, and soon after Henry Ford started mass producing cars to usher in the automobile age. Over the next century, numerous safety features were invented for use on automobiles: safety glass, turn signals, safety cage construction, three-point seat belts, anti-lock brakes, airbags, and rudimentary collision avoidance systems in the early 2000s. While self-

---

[5] Various sources listed on the following Wikipedia page:
https://en.wikipedia.org/wiki/Nicolas-Joseph_Cugnot

driving and accident-free vehicles may soon be a reality, even today about one person dies for every 100 million miles driven in the US due to factors such as speeding, alcohol impairment, and driver error.[6] This means that it has taken us about 250 years to develop relatively safe vehicles, but we are still not immune to the effects of human carelessness.

Charles Babbage is credited with designing the first mechanical computer in 1834[7]. Nearly 200 years have passed, and the list of improvements to computers is exhaustive. Yet designing hardware, writing software and configuring these devices are primarily human responsibilities. And just as humans make mistakes while driving that result in vehicle accidents, mistakes made while developing or installing software can result in vulnerabilities that can be exploited by hackers. There are numerous software development tools available to help write and test software to improve its performance and reliability. Unfortunately, these same testing tools can be used by hackers after the software is published to find errors known as bugs. Any bugs found by hackers rather than the original developers could be (and quickly are) used to take advantage of user devices. While software has become more advanced and computers far more powerful, some old software code components and programming languages are still prevalent and weaknesses are discovered every day. At the same time, new technologies are adopted rapidly without considering the potential vulnerabilities or unintentional data sharing they may introduce. And all the while, users can disable key security features, use weak passwords, and install untested software on devices that make them more susceptible to hackers.

If we parallel the same technological timeline it took to provide drivers with safer automobiles, we may have about fifty more years until self-healing networks and attack-resistance technologies are powerful enough to completely prevent human error from compromising our digital devices. Granted, many of the safety improvements in automobiles were only possible because of computers, so this prediction may be little more than a good cocktail party topic of discussion. While we might all hope it doesn't take that long until our digital lives are perfectly secure, in the interim we

[6] Traffic Safety Facts, May 2018, DOT HS 812 542, National Highway Traffic Safety Administration, Department of Transportation.
https://crashstats.nhtsa.dot.gov/Api/Public/ViewPublication/812542

[7] The Babbage Engine, pulled 4 March 2018, The Computer History Museum.
http://www.computerhistory.org/babbage/engines/

can better protect ourselves by understanding the enemy and what they are after.

Common Hacking Techniques

Criminals have always found ways to steal from others by either bypassing weak security mechanisms or exploiting our innate trust of authority figures, friends or colleagues. Cyber criminals follow this same approach by exploiting vulnerabilities in software or tricking people operating connected devices.

For example, when hackers find a vulnerability in a single computer in an office, it can be used to get into the remainder of the organization's network. This process usually requires reconnaissance and a series of successful attacks against vulnerabilities in various layers of a network's security implementation and is usually a complex process. But if done properly, in a manner that is slow and methodical enough, these types of attacks are very hard to detect without advanced intrusion detection tools. Other attacks are successful by using stolen log-in credentials or going after vulnerabilities in web interfaces to data that is not very well protected.

However, a much more reliable approach is via a human inside the target network. Many recent widely-reported attacks were accomplished by *phishing*, which is a technique that uses seemingly official or intriguing-looking emails that contain malicious attachments or links to hostile servers impersonating legitimate web sites.

While fishermen cast nets to catch many small fish, hackers regularly use phishing tactics to target huge pools of users with specially-crafted emails about online shopping bargains, sex, or controversial subjects. The attackers use email address libraries or generators to target thousands of users at a time, and many phishing emails are caught by spam or malware filters. But if the email is crafted well enough, it may make it through any automated security tool guarding the user's inbox. If the user then opens the email and clicks on the included link or attachment, the malware may be able to trick the user into installing additional malware tools or, as seen recently, encrypt all user data on their device for ransom. These phishing attacks have been so successful on computers in schools, hospitals, and offices around the world that the frequency of these attacks continues to increase.

Rather than casting nets, some fishermen use spears to target a single fish. Similarly, *spearphishing* attacks go after a specific person with tailored, personally-addressed emails to increase the likelihood of success. If any of these attacks are successful on a device that is somehow connected to an organization's network, the sensitive data available to that person is also put at risk.

To best accomplish a spearphishing attack, hackers research victim organizations to find personnel most likely to have high-level access to the desired information. When the best target is identified—perhaps an executive, network administrator, or other insider close to the desired data—an attacker might use publicly-available information found on the organization's web page, social media sites or press releases to find associations, interests, and perhaps even more detailed information that could be useful in crafting an intriguing email. The attacker then sends this customized email to the unwitting employee. The 'hook is set' when the employee opens a malicious attachment or clicks a link to a hostile web server that has been prepared to exploit a vulnerability on the employee's device. And since vulnerabilities are found in common consumer and corporate software products sometimes before a fix is even available, some of these spearfishing attacks can be devastating due to the target's position in the organization.

Recent Attacks

We could dedicate an entire book to detailing notable attacks against victim companies in numerous industries, but a single recent court case against foreign hackers is enough to illustrate why you should immediately adopt a rigorous defensive posture for your organization. In November 2017, the US Government filed an indictment against three Chinese hackers for a series of network intrusions beginning in 2011.[8] While working for Boyusec, an "Internet security" firm in Guangzhou, China, these hackers allegedly stole massive amounts of sensitive data from several top-tier technology and finance companies.

Beginning in 2011, the hackers targeted the financial sector by gaining access to and reconfiguring a corporate email server belonging to Moody's Analytics. The hackers configured the server to covertly auto-forward all emails to and from a prominent employee to a secondary email account under the hackers' exclusive control. Over the next few years, the hackers were able to use this secondary account to read all of this employee's

---

[8] U.S. Charges Three Chinese Hackers Who Work at Internet Security Firm for Hacking Three Corporations for Commercial Advantage, Monday, November 27, 2017. Downloaded from:
   https://www.justice.gov/opa/press-release/file/1013866/download

proprietary and confidential economic assessments and findings on a variety of economic research areas.

In 2014, these same hackers targeted Siemens, an international conglomerate with interests in a variety of sectors to include financial services, building technologies, mobility operations, healthcare, transportation, power systems, and energy management. Once inside the Siemens network, the hackers spent the next year exfiltrating 407 gigabytes (23 million pages!) of intellectual property about Siemens's energy, technology and transportation ventures.

And in 2015 and 2016, the hackers targeted Trimble, a California-based company developing global positioning technologies used on mobile devices around the world. The hackers were able to steal 275 megabytes of sensitive product designs and test data that took years of research and development time and millions of dollars for Trimble to amass.

The Boyusec hackers used spearphishing to target individuals inside each company and then deposited malware on vulnerable systems. Using these modified systems, the hackers were able to operate for years without detection. While the damage done to each of these companies listed in this indictment may be significant, it is quite possible that Boyusec might employ other hackers who could have compromised many more companies around the world using similar tactics and techniques.

This is just one case against three hackers who were actually caught and charged for severely damaging the reputation and business advantage of three valuable companies. The number of businesses reporting similar cyber attacks is growing yet catching hackers in the act is incredibly difficult without adequate resources. When you consider that companies like Siemens and Moody's likely had robust information technology (IT) teams supporting their operations but remained compromised without being detected for several years, this single case should convince you that the enemy is just as capable and motivated of doing significant damage to any organization, large or small. The important lesson here is that even if you have an IT department, it's not only their responsibility to know your enemy. Anyone in your organization can be a spearphishing target. Even you.

Executive Summaries

Andrew Grove was president and later chairman of the Intel Corporation during the 1980s and 1990s. He captured the essence of his leadership style there in the title of his popular management book: <u>Only</u>

The Paranoid Survive. While leading Intel through the growth of the computer industry, Grove realized that competition was fierce and only a keen sense of attention to detail and keeping an eye out for potential areas of failure helped him transform Intel from a memory chip maker on the brink of bankruptcy to the multi-billion-dollar microprocessor industry leader. Paranoia generally has a negative connotation, but in cyber war, it's a completely rational perspective that could help prevent disaster. When you realize that others are actively trying to steal your treasures, it won't take long to develop a healthy sense of paranoia about the security of your organization's data.

There are many cybersecurity and threat analysis reports available on line. I recommend you go to your favorite search engine and type "Cyber Threat Report 20XX" (fill in the year) to find reports from commercial security vendors and government agencies from around the world.[9] Most are free to read at the executive summary level, and some may be free even at the more technical level. Some reports released by government-funded agencies or non-profit organizations are provided to help improve the common cybersecurity environment, while others from security vendors will normally highlight their company's security tools as a solution to mitigate the threats noted in the report. My recommendation is to read as many reports as time allows to get a general understanding of the current environment. If you are responsible for allocating your IT department's budget, you might consider the cost of technical reports or those tailored for your industry to be a wise investment.

Some of the facts in these reports that should pique your interest include the method of attack, the scope of damage done, and the costs of recovery. Numerous well-executed hacks have been accomplished with very little effort from hackers on the opposite side of the globe, and there is no end in sight. While you may now be thinking there's little more to be done other than buying cyber disaster insurance, consider that some insurance policies may not cover human error or negligence (for example, using weak passwords, falling for spearfishing attacks, etc.). Your organization must be proactive to limit its exposure to cyber war. But where do you begin? In the next chapter, we'll return to Sun Tzu and learn more about ourselves.

---

[9] Refer to Appendix 6.

CHAPTER 4

Know Yourself

What's In Your Castle?

Several years ago, IT managers regularly used the basic architecture of a medieval castle to help explain their security model. Traditional castles were surrounded by motes filled with water, built with high thick walls and featured complex mazes leading to the inner rooms containing the treasure. Simple networks had a similar design with firewalls, limited access methods, and complex passwords to protect sensitive data. While the castle analogy is considered a dated and simplistic security model by modern IT standards, we can still use this analogy for demonstration purposes.

Imagine trying to draw a diagram of your current *cyber castle*. At the center of your castle is the data you want to protect, whether it's banking transactions, proprietary company data, or sensitive personal information. Everything around that data—the castle walls and doorways—are the security tools on all devices that are capable of providing or preventing access to that data. These tools might be analogous to a door or window on your castle wall, some like small portholes and others huge gateways connected by a drawbridge over the protective moat. Imagine trying to inventory all of the computers and personnel who have access to these computers in your organization. Would it take you a long time to capture the details of all devices in your local office? How long would it take if this applied to other distant branch offices in your organization? They may be far away, but you must consider them a part of your castle.

If you work from home, consider your daily routine. If you're like most people you'll check your phone, turn on the television, read the news on line, and perhaps send out some emails. How many Internet-connected devices do you use every morning? Is your television cable box connected to your home network? Your game console? Maybe even your refrigerator or other connected smart devices?

If Sun Tzu were preparing for cyber war, he would feel compelled as the commanding general to spend a lot of time examining all of the interconnected devices in the castle to truly "know himself." He may look at an old computer in the corner and wonder who is still using it and for what purpose. He would wonder why certain games and social networking apps were installed on company phones, and he might wonder why the conference room's AV amplifier was plugged in to the network. But that is exactly the right way of thinking that would help protect your organization. The next few sections will explore some of the information you should know to understand your exposure to the cyber war. While the guidance here isn't exhaustive, the areas discussed will hopefully open your eyes to some potential vulnerabilities and help you to better prioritize where you spend valuable resources to protect what is most important. So let's begin there, with what is most important.

Mission-Supporting Treasures

Because organizations have unique leadership structures and different goals in their respective marketplaces, each organization has a unique mission and thus a different concept of what resources are most important to that mission. Each will have many treasures with some being more important to their operations than others, and thus some should be considered more valuable. The most valuable treasures are those that the organization would be unable to operate without, while other treasures may be sensitive or confidential enough to negatively impact operations should they be lost or stolen. The treasure may be physical, like money in the bank or inventory on the shelf, but since most businesses use computers to automate or expedite key operations, the electronic records and systems used to process these physical goods should also be considered treasure to be protected. Treasures may also have a higher replacement cost than their actual worth or may carry liabilities in the form of fees or penalties should they be disclosed. The following table lists a few sample organizations and possible treasures.

Table 1. Mission Supporting Treasures

Organization	Treasure
Any business	Cash in bank accounts, payroll accounts, etc.
Any business	Customer contact information
Any business	Customer billing information (account numbers or credit card numbers)
Any business	"Frequent Buyer Card" member database
Any business	Business plans or strategies
Any business	Public web page
Any business	Email system and email archives
Manufacturing business	Product designs, drawings or schematics
Construction company	Blueprints, plans, supplier contracts, etc.
Software Company	Computer source code
Photographer, Videographer or Media Company	Digital assets like videos, photographs, drawings and graphics
Bank or Investment Firm	Financial transaction histories
Law firm	Client lists, briefs, files, findings, etc.
Hospital or Doctor's office	HIPA files (digital health records, etc.)
Restaurant	Reservation systems, point of sale systems, recipes, menus, food vendor contracts, etc.
Professional musician	Recordings, sheet music, digital assets
News outlet (online, print, television)	Video or audio recordings, articles and web pages
Retail, Grocery or Convenience Store	Physical products being sold or serviced, inventory records, vendor contracts, etc.
Security Company	Remote monitoring systems, communications with field units
Online content provider	Digital assets and un-interrupted connectivity

Spend some time to define all of your organization's treasures and consider the relative value of each treasure. The examples above should trigger some ideas for considering all the treasures and systems that support your organization. If you are unsure about the potential liabilities for data in your organization's area of operations, do some research on that subject as soon as practical. The more time you spend understanding all of the treasures in your castle, the better prepared you will be to make strategic decisions about protecting those treasures and ultimately, defending your entire organization.

Once you have a good understanding of the full scope of your treasures, you should grow curious about where those treasures are located, how you are protecting them, and who has regular access to these treasures. If you're not curious, go back to your list and think about what would happen if you lost control of any of these treasures.

The IT Crowd

If you are relatively new to your organization, you likely inherited a computer infrastructure that was built by others over several years or even decades. If you have been in your organization a long time, you might notice that some of the connected devices installed years ago might still be in use. Either way, all of the devices that are connected to your organization's infrastructure are now part of your castle. What you don't know about these devices is that some—perhaps many—of these devices may only be as secure as paper-thin doors with easy-to-pick locks. Other devices may introduce vulnerabilities like cracks or gaping holes in your castle walls, putting your treasure at risk. Like castle wall maintenance, keeping your IT infrastructure up to date is (or should be) a key part of your annual operations and maintenance budget. Does your organization have an IT department resourced for implementing these responsibilities? While some may be quick to consider the task of updating computers and procuring online services as strictly IT department responsibilities, most organizations don't have sufficient resources allocated for a robust IT department.

While many organizational IT departments are staffed with hard-working and helpful technicians, a common theme among these experts is that they are under-trained and over-worked, yet expected to provide bullet-proof mission-supporting service at all times. Another common theme is that most things in cybersecurity ultimately balance user convenience against security, and when the decision makers don't have an understanding of the risks, convenience generally comes first. In the typical organization, everyone on the staff is using some service or device that is somehow connected to the treasure. These tools range from cloud-based email accounts that can be accessed from nearly anywhere to a network storage device full of company data located in some forgotten office closet. And yet, the organization's leadership expects their minimal IT staff to properly defend the castle from all attacks against these devices and services.

A recent trend is to hire a CISO, or a Chief Information Security Officer, to help an organization prioritize its cybersecurity efforts. The CISO should have a solid understanding of the organization's mission and treasures and will be given the authority and resources to implement all of the required defenses. As a C-suite executive, the CISO will be able to align security expenditures with business priorities and have the full support of other C-suite executives to implement the required security measures. While this may be a cost-effective position for a company with an adequate budget, most organizations might think the average salary for a well-qualified CISO is too expensive. Like all business decisions, the expense has to be worth the reward or significantly cheaper than any potential risks. How much spending would make your organization best prepared for cyber war? Can you afford to spend more on IT to enhance cybersecurity? Were you contemplating spending less? Or are current financial conditions forcing you to try other initiatives to secure your treasure without spending money on additional cybersecurity tools and personnel?

These questions bring us back to the theme of this book: because you know your organization's mission and treasure, you can be more effective in helping to defend the castle by following Sun Tzu's example. It's time to know ourselves by walking the castle walls. If you've got an IT staff, a complex network and lots of computers, your castle should be pretty well mapped out, and the staff should be able to explain the infrastructure and security implementation in sufficient detail. You may even have a certified cybersecurity expert on staff happy to be your guide in the hopes of securing executive-level support for some important initiatives. Regardless of their capabilities, have your IT team lead take you on a tour of your organization's IT infrastructure using information in the following sections to shape your questions. If you don't have an IT staff, then you'll have to walk the castle by yourself (and consider hiring some IT experts when you finish). Either way, walking the walls should clarify the scope of vulnerabilities in your organization so that you'll be better prepared to make cybersecurity decisions.

Walking the Castle Walls

Most leaders enjoy having an excuse to get out of their office to talk with their staff and get a better sense of the day-to-day operations, but be prepared to devote as much time as possible to walking your castle walls. This step may take a seemingly excessive amount of time or be at what some executives might consider an "in the weeds" level of detail, so you may think about delegating this to someone else. However, getting you actively engaged in cybersecurity is the sole purpose of this book, and I urge you to consider this as both a perfect opportunity to personally explore your IT infrastructure and to ask about everyone's understanding of their part of castle defense.

If your organization is large and you have an IT guide to help you, consider starting with just a portion of the infrastructure. If you're reviewing a small organization's infrastructure alone, you should endeavor to inventory every applicable device. The key thing as you explore your castle is to pay attention to what your staff is saying about cybersecurity, but don't hesitate to ask about things they're *not* saying. Ask questions such as "*why is it done this way?*" and "*who performs our computer operations, maintenance or support tasks?*" as you explore your castle. Ensuring the cybersecurity of any device also includes ensuring physical security, so observe whether server cabinets and server rooms are locked and smaller computers have any anti-theft devices.

Using your organization's mission-essential treasures you identified earlier in the chapter as a guide, review the systems that store any data related to these treasures. For systems not in your organization's direct control, like web-based or cloud-based tools, determine the vendor and review as much information as you can about their services. If the systems are all physically in your organization, you should have access to the specifics of the devices to include make, model, age, and operating system version. Most of these devices will be connected to your network, but ensure your review includes all data-processing devices whether they're connected or not.

Next, review the devices that have a role in your organization's daily communications. Inventory all things like point of sale systems, desktop and laptop computers, land-line phones, cell phones, and tablets with as much detail as possible. If you or anyone else in your organization conducts business on their personal devices, consider those devices as part of the inventory as well, even though without existing user policies you may not be legally able to ask for specifics of their make, model or operating system. Inventory all other systems that communicate from within your organization to the outside world, including VOIP (Voice Over IP) network phones that rely on internet connections.

If you have a web site, review all of the details about the web server. Your organization should know where the site is hosted, on what operating system, and what web services are running on your web site. Be aware of any databases or management tools used on your site and find out how changes are made to the web server (for example, does someone log in via a web interface, or are there a series of development/test/production staging servers that are connected to your organization's network).

Finally, ensure you review any credit card processing and verification systems and any "connected devices" like copiers, scanners, or other "Internet of Things" devices like security cameras and smart appliances. Some televisions may have "smart" features such as video conferencing, video streaming, voice recognition, or screen sharing. While connected copiers and TVs may have seemingly innocuous features, imagine if hackers got access to every document you scanned, listened to the sensitive discussions you had in the conference room, or broke in to your network via a wifi-enabled weather unit someone mounted on the window.

If you are thinking you don't know enough about computers to perform a sufficient review, it is truly time to educate yourself by growing curious about the walls protecting your treasure. Our society isn't becoming less connected or less digital, so ignoring the basics of the connected devices that are so critical to your operation is like not caring about the locks on your doors or tracking who has been issued keys. The goal of this review is for you to learn how your organization will react to the next big cyber vulnerability. For example, if an emergency update was posted to fix a dangerous vulnerability for an operating system or software package, would you be able to quickly determine how many of your devices needed the patch? If a majority of your devices needed the update, how long would it take to patch them all? Remember that you are ultimately responsible for your organization, so you should understand everything about how your castle is built, to include how it communicates with the outside world.

Castle Communications

The network in your organization not only connects the devices to each other, but it is a distinct, virtual avenue from your organization to the global internet. This avenue can be a limited resource, with strict limits on monthly data usage, or it can be seemingly limitless with more than enough capacity for all of your needs. It may provide strong protections from outside intrusions and total privacy for those using the network inside your organization, or it may provide neither. Unfortunately, your network could also be a direct connection to anyone around the globe interested in plundering your digital treasures.

Begin your understanding of the scope of your network by learning how the devices you reviewed in the previous section are connected to it. As you walk around the castle (your home or office), think of everything that is plugged in to the network or connected via wifi as a potential hole in your castle wall. Are there tens of devices on your network, or thousands? Are devices added whenever needed and without control, or is there a regulated process for adding new devices to the network to ensure security? Are there any security controls for keeping devices updated, and if so, when a device fails to meet these security requirements, is it blocked from the network? Remember, every device allowed on the network provides a new access point for potential hackers.

If there is a wifi network in your organization, is it open or encrypted? How many users know the password to the wifi network? This would be a good time to review the client list or connected devices tables of your wifi router to get a sense of what devices are connected. You might be surprised to see how many devices are using your wifi network, and if this network is somehow connected to your treasure, you'll be concerned that all of these random devices are also connected to those treasures.

If your organization regularly shares data with off-site locations, learn how these processes take place and how the data is secured during transit. Determine if there are dedicated circuits to any off-site locations, or whether you connect via a Virtual Private Network (VPN) tunneled through the internet. If you do use a VPN, learn what you can about how this connection is implemented and maintained. If you only send internal communications to other locations via email, determine if security measures like encryption are in place to protect any sensitive or proprietary data.

Finally, determine if any security appliances are on your network such as: web filters/proxies, firewalls, intrusion detection/prevention systems, load balancers, anti-virus tools, email/spam tools, file servers, etc. Depending on your network's design, you may have some or all of these devices and more.

By now, you should have a better understanding of the devices and network your organization relies upon, but you should also know more about who in your organization is actually responsible for protecting your treasure.

Reviewing the Troops

Sun Tzu's <u>The Art of War</u> contains guidance on the use of spies to learn everything about an enemy. Sun Tzu noted that some information could be released to others for broadcasting strength or feigning weakness, while other secrets required sometimes harsh (deadly) protection measures to ensure victory. While his explanation of using spies is focused on warfare, many of the same concepts could be applied to business intelligence (except the deadly part, of course).

Learning about business competitors is an essential part of establishing market dominance, as is protecting your organization's proprietary information from the competition. Recalling once again your organization's treasures, think about everyone who has access to them and what damage could be done if competitors or criminals obtained access. In warfare, operational security is used to maintain control of and prevent unauthorized disclosure of the military's treasures. In essence, military intelligence and business intelligence are closely related, and in both instances operational security could reduce the amount of information that the competitor would find beneficial.

Common information protection mechanisms used in today's modern military are classification and access controls. Some information that is deemed valuable enough will be entrusted only to those who truly need the information for their operations, while more basic information can be shared with everyone. The rationale for classifying information to limit access to a specific subset of the organization draws from a number of factors to include the sources and methods used to collect the information, the risk of losing control of that information, and the trustworthiness of those protecting the information. You should have similar concerns about the information you previously identified as your organizational treasures, and who actually needs to have access to those treasures.

At the most basic level, the free flow of information between all levels of an organization is a benefit. Good ideas can come from the personnel working "in the trenches" and leadership's new strategies can be shared to help motivate the entire staff. Realistically though, some information doesn't need to be shared with everyone in the organization. For example, medical information about all employees might be needed for an insurance policy, but it shouldn't be shared to satisfy everyone's curiosity. Similarly, personally identifiable information (PII as it is commonly called) like home addresses and social security numbers must be protected by law from unauthorized disclosure. Information about the development of a new technology that could provide a competitive advantage would obviously need to be better protected than a notice about the company picnic, so clearly every organization has a requirement to protect at least some of their information from those who don't have a need to know.

Does your organization have any rules on limiting access to sensitive information? When you consider the devices on the network to be the access points to your treasure, think about the people in your organization using these devices. Does each person have the same access to all of the files as everyone else? How do you ensure access is limited, and are there any mechanisms in place to log and audit each instance of access? Does every employee have access to all of the devices on the network, or only those needed for their current duties? Since we are talking about the data representing your organization's treasure, how do you know if someone made a copy of the data somewhere else on the network, or emailed a copy somewhere to make it easier to work from home or on a business trip?

If your organization has a web page, you are likely trying to communicate with current and potential customers. You are also communicating with your competitors, so you should review what information you are sharing and how you are ensuring it reaches only those you intend. Any limited access areas of your web presence should be continuously monitored to limit abuse and unauthorized disclosure, and former clients who no longer need access should be removed. What other similar online services or systems are managed by your personnel?

While walking the walls, you likely identified some systems like email or cloud storage services used by your organization. Who in your organization is responsible for administering them? For example, determine who has the master account user name and password for the service's monthly billing and account management duties. Does anyone else have administrator access, or are you entirely dependent on a single individual to be available whenever needed? How many people are in your IT department? Are they happy working there, or are they looking for a new job? Would your organization be at risk if a key player was suddenly unavailable? If you need someone to reset your mail account password at 3:00 AM when you are on a business trip in Tokyo, who does this task, and would they do it from home on the same personal computer they use to watch cat videos and download random software from the internet?

Finally, how well trained is everyone for cyber war? Does everyone in your organization know how to identify a phishing email? Are you and your key staff on guard for potential spearphishing attacks? Or do they not know what those words mean? Are all of the personnel you entrust with your treasure aware of the information's sensitivity and the risks of losing access? Everyone in the organization has a responsibility to help maintain cybersecurity, from the technicians maintaining the systems to the sales employee checking email on their smartphone. Everyone plays a part.

Feeling Lost?

Wondering why you're walking around looking at computers and checking the locks on server rooms? Do you have more questions about your castle than you do answers? You may have come to a few of the following conclusions:

1. Your organization has only a few devices and doesn't operate on an office network
2. Your personnel are well trained and fully capable of detecting and repelling cyber attacks
3. Your organization operates a complex network connecting a vast array of devices
4. Your organization uses many third-party services for email, cloud apps and storage, web hosting, etc.
5. Your organization relies on a relatively small IT team to build and manage the network while defending the treasures
6. Your personnel need more training, more resources, and more help to keep the organization operating securely
7. Your organization's leadership team needs advice on how to best realign resources to improve cybersecurity

If you agreed only with conclusions 1 and 2, you might be feeling that your organization's cybersecurity posture is strong enough or isn't vulnerable to cyber attack. While this may be true for very few organizations, most organizations will agree with conclusions 3 through 7. And even though many would come to these same conclusions, leadership in businesses and governments around the world are trusting (hoping?) that their IT infrastructure is impervious to criminal acts or disasters of any kind.

Trust No One

President Ronald Regan frequently used a Russian proverb during nuclear disarmament talks with the Soviet Union: "trust but verify." While we want to *trust* that our employees care just as much about our organization's treasure as we do, we certainly can't be certain that mistakes won't be made. But without years of experience, how do non-IT leaders *verify* what the IT department is doing on the infrastructure is correct and secure, or *trust* what others are doing with our treasure on their devices? We certainly can't trust that hackers around the world won't try to break any security we have in place, and (so far) no automated security tools can fully verify network security against all kinds of attacks. "Trust but verify" alone won't succeed in cyber war, but any leader who doesn't trust their team won't fully earn their loyalty or support.

So how do you instill a healthy sense of cyber paranoia throughout the organization without ruining morale? While Sun Tzu's extreme measures for keeping secrets won't help you, perhaps the manner in which today's military uses intelligence can provide some guidance.

CHAPTER 5

The Military Intelligence Process

Military Intelligence

Sun Tzu discussed the use of spies to determine enemy troop strength and obtain updates on unit movement, but he didn't truly define military intelligence. According to the Department of Defense's (DoD) Joint Publication 2-0, modern military ***intelligence*** is that which is produced by analyzing information or raw data in the context of an operational environment.[10] The key here is that information and raw data (like troop strength or location) need to be further analyzed in the context of the situation before it can be considered intelligence. This is a subtle distinction, but some information may not have enough meaning unless it is combined with other information about the circumstances and environment.

To help understand the concepts of military intelligence, this chapter will use a simplistic military scenario to emphasize key concepts. Imagine you are the commander of a missile defense unit with the mission of defending your base from the enemy's truck-mounted short-range missiles. Your ultimate goal is to protect your assets against enemy aggression, either by surviving the attack or deterring a launch altogether. As a commander, having the best possible intelligence about the operational environment would give you a tremendous advantage to help achieve that goal. But if you are an artillery officer rather than a trained intelligence officer, you may not know what "intelligence" truly means or how to create it.

Before calling your buddy in the intelligence unit, imagine that you want to learn the characteristics of the missiles and the truck-mounted launchers. Suppose you were able to observe the enemy's missile trucks during one of

---

[10] Download the entire Joint Publication 2-0, Intelligence from http://www.jcs.mil/Portals/36/Documents/Doctrine/pubs/jp2_0.pdf

their field exercises. You noticed things like the missile trucks' average top speed, measurements of the tightest turns they made, and how the trucks performed poorly in the snow or mud. While these facts may seem interesting, alone they won't help you understand when a missile launch might occur. Consider how meaningful it would be if you knew exactly where the trucks and missiles were stored, details of the roads connecting these locations to possible launch sites close enough to your territory, and specifics about the weather in the area.

A robust military intelligence office would be able to collect information from a variety of sources to determine the most likely routes the missile launchers would utilize around the year. For example, some unpaved roads might be too muddy during the rainy season or packed with snow during the winter. Some paved roads might be completely inaccessible by the missile trucks due to tight turns or narrow bridges. As the commander in charge of the missile defense mission, this information would give you a greater appreciation for all of the indications of an impending launch, to include how much time it might take for the trucks to reach all of the likely launch sites. Clearly any process that produced a concise summary of this kind of information from many different sources would be extremely helpful to you as the commander.

The Intelligence Process

The Department of Defense's Joint Publication 2-0 details the process that commanders and intelligence analysts follow together in order to create the intelligence needed to support the mission. While the commander might not be a military intelligence expert, he or she is actively engaged in this process to ensure mission success because the best decisions are made with as much knowledge and feedback as possible.

The following diagram shows the cyclical process used to continuously provide relevant information to decision makers. The process is followed in a cycle in order to adapt to new enemy techniques or capabilities and to assess the effects of military activities against the enemy.

Samuel D. Bass

Figure 1. The Military Intelligence Process

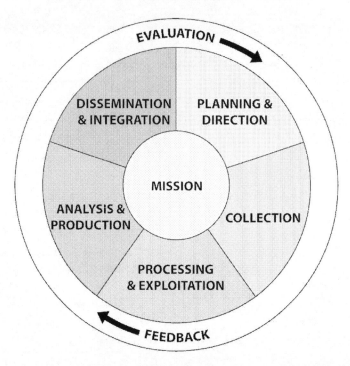

(Diagram adapted from DoD Joint Publication 2-0, 22 Oct 2013)

Mission

'Mission' is at the center of the diagram. For the military commander, this is the most important concept as it drives all decisions about resources and activities. For most businesses, the mission is essentially to make money. For government agencies, it is to protect and provide the common good for its people. And for a family home, the mission is to provide a happy and secure environment. The mission should guide any leader's decisions, so a clear understanding of an organization's mission is the essential first step in this process. Here are some sample organizations and missions:

Table 2. Sample Missions

Organization	Mission
Computer hardware manufacturing company	Sell computer products for maximum profit
Local Government Business Development Agency	Maximize jobs and tax revenue for city operations
Non-profit healthcare provider	Provide free medical care to maximum patients
Chain restaurant	Sell food and drink for maximum profit
Corner hardware store	Sell hardware products for maximum profit
Family Household	Provide a safe and secure environment for all inhabitants

Not only do the above organizations (and likely all others) rely on financial resources, each organization has a unique mission focus. While the above missions are watered down for simplicity, there are obviously many factors that go in to truly understanding an organization's mission. For example, one computer company's mission may be to sell many cheap computers for a little profit on each, while another may sell fewer specialized computers for a higher unit profit. A non-profit organization may conduct its fundraising on-line and another may rely on corporate sponsorships. Your organization's mission will be unique in both outcome and organizational approach, and therefore your cybersecurity priorities will likely differ from most other organizations. And that is precisely the point of this book: you must take an active role in defining your cybersecurity posture in the context of your mission, just as the military commander is active in directing the intelligence process for a specific operational environment.

As we continue with the missile defense scenario, let's agree that your mission is simply to *deter enemy missile attacks.* This is only an extremely simplified summary rather than a full mission statement, which might include more details about deterrence, readiness, implementing anti-missile weapons, or negating the missile's lethality with better bunkers, etc.[11]

---

[11] See a sample mission statement from the Missile Defense Agency found on their website: http://www.mda.mil/about/mission.html

Planning and Direction

With a clear understanding of the mission, the commander can decide what data would help make better decisions about various actions. In our scenario, you ask for a detailed intelligence report about the enemy's missile trucks. Knowing who makes the trucks might provide information about their capabilities and performance, but additional information such as parts suppliers and known reliability issues will deepen your understanding of future observations. If intelligence analysts see a new shipment of truck tires arrive, you might direct the collection of information about the company supplying the tires, where they were produced, and whether the enemy is improving their off-road capabilities to make more launch sites available. Changes like this will often drive commanders to occasionally ask the intelligence analysts to "dig deeper" to find new vulnerabilities or opportunities.

Another important point is prioritizing these intelligence collection activities. If there are only a few intelligence analysts available to conduct all gathering and reporting, prioritization must be applied to ensure they're not tracking down tire manufacturers when they should be watching where the launchers are moving. If too many things are equally important for the analysis staff, the intelligence unit may have to ask for assistance from outside sources like commercial satellite imagery companies or reports from paid think-tanks.

In summary, both the commander and the supporting intelligence unit have a clear understanding of the mission and are able to direct intelligence activities to better know the enemy. The commander can also use this planning and direction phase to direct changes to training programs, coordinate better defensive measures, and devise plans to protect valuable assets from known threats. Finally, the commander is involved in guiding the intelligence staff's activities and is properly prioritizing their efforts.

Collection

Once a commander has set the priorities for the needed intelligence, the process of collecting the data can begin. Depending on the intelligence needed, the raw data can be collected from numerous sources. These sources can include visual observations, data from remote sensors, or information from other organizations. And once again, limited collection resources must be prioritized for deployment in accordance with the relative importance to the mission. If the commander can only get regular satellite imagery for some of the truck garages, the coverage may be directed over only those closest to the probable launch points. The driving factor for these prioritization questions is always (of course) the direct applicability to the mission.

If the commander has a new priority for intelligence and the collection tools aren't available, the decision to procure more capability will be measured against the risk to mission failure. In our scenario, total satellite coverage of all known missile truck garages would reduce the risk of an unexpected attack, but acquiring more satellite time or placing new assets in orbit is extremely expensive.

Linking the procurement decision to improve collection capabilities with supporting the mission is no different in the intelligence process than it is in similar business intelligence decisions, like buying marketing research reports or customer contact databases. The ability to confidently make these decisions comes from understanding the mission and knowing if the costs could help improve the unit's ability to achieve its mission.

Processing and Exploitation

Once the data is collected, analysts will convert it into forms that can be used by others. The processing may be done for not only the commander who initially asked for the intelligence, but perhaps for decision makers in other departments or intelligence analysts who will combine multiple sources for other collection priorities. Depending on the source of the data collected, the analysts reviewing it may have more or less work to make it applicable to their organization's mission needs.

Furthermore, some of the processing may be automated or sent to another organization for processing. This is particularly true for high-volume raw data that would be too work-intensive or monotonous for human analysts. Examples from the business world may include analysis of foot traffic data to determine which stores get more customers, what areas are the busiest, or web server log reviews to determine the average browsing time per customer of an important web page. Processing this kind of data might be too time intensive or beyond the capabilities of your organization's staff, but an outside analytics firm might be able to conduct this analysis at a reasonable cost.

In our ongoing missile defense scenario, because your assigned intelligence experts might not have any experience with assessing missile launch performance, telemetry data captured during an enemy test launch would be forwarded to space launch experts outside of the organization for further processing. In this way, your missile defense unit's intelligence analysts could spend their time on other priorities like analyzing surveillance video of the enemy's launch preparation procedures to understand the indications of an imminent launch.

Analysis and Production

Once the information is processed, it is fused into final intelligence products. In this phase, multiple experts will summarize the analysis of their area of expertise so it can be combined to meet the organization's needs. All of the raw data from numerous sources and in different forms was analyzed by numerous experts and converted into intelligence that can be presented in an understandable format. These final intelligence products could be in the form of executive summaries, detailed studies, briefings, or training materials. These products must all be tailor-made for the end user since leadership may use these products to make strategic decisions, financial officers may approve purchases, and front-line personnel may alter their procedures as a result of the content of these intelligence products.

Just as the processing may be outsourced to others, the analysis and report production tasks could be accomplished by someone outside the organization. As long as the resulting report is usable in the context of the mission requirements, quality reports may be produced by a third party. Note that the term "usable" will be entirely up to the consumer of the reports. If the mission commander can't use the reports to improve unit operations, the time and effort to collect this information and create the reports has been wasted. Similarly in business, if a CEO doesn't understand an executive-level report enough to help make decisions about mitigating threats to the company's mission or important data assets, the reports aren't worth the cost. If the reports for decision makers are too technical or aren't focused on the mission, they will be relegated to the other subordinate departments as though they are irrelevant to those making strategic decisions. While in some cases this may be useful (for example, an analysis of new hacking techniques that the CEO doesn't need to understand but the network security team could use to bolster defenses), care must be taken to ensure everyone gets the needed information at the appropriate level of detail. That is precisely why the commander is involved in guiding the intelligence process: decision makers must be able to fully understand current and emerging risks to the mission.

In our scenario, the completed missile defense report would provide all of the current intelligence about the missile trucks, the missiles and warheads. Effective reports would give the commander enough information about the indications of an impending launch, an estimate of how long it will take for the missile trucks to arrive at the necessary launch site, and what friendly assets the enemy is likely targeting. These reports could be used by personnel in the satellite operations center to understand how quickly they need to react to imagery showing the signs of an impending launch, used in resource allocation meetings to procure anti-missile technology, or guide decisions on moving assets to better-protected bunkers.

Dissemination and Integration

When intelligence reports are created, they must be delivered in a timely manner to the intended consumer in the unit. For units operating in different time-zones around the world, this may be a challenge to accomplish in a timely manner depending on the immediacy and available communications. Additionally, if personnel are unfamiliar with a new threat to the mission, they may need to be trained by experts to help integrate mitigations into their daily operations. If all personnel don't understand why this intelligence is important, it might be ignored at the cost of increasing risk to the mission.

Another important part of integrating intelligence into operations is that of follow-up and verification. If some portions of a large and diverse unit have yet to adjust their operations but the decision makers are under the assumption that everyone is complying with the new guidance, there may be no overall reduction in risk to the mission, or no reaction to competitor advancement. While verification may be obvious in some departments, this can be time consuming and difficult without adequate tools. Additionally, if personnel in the field aren't complying with new procedures, one possible reason may be that the reports weren't understood by the target audience or they don't understand the risk to the mission. The reports must be effective in communicating the intelligence to those who need it the most.

Once again as the missile defense unit commander, you will want to ensure that the reports were distributed to the appropriate personnel, checklists and procedures were modified, and users trained so that the unit is ready to properly react to the earliest possible indications of an impending launch.

Evaluation and Feedback

Evaluating the quality of the intelligence produced doesn't just happen at the completion of this process. As depicted in the earlier diagram, it is critical that evaluation and feedback occur continuously throughout the process. If a new event occurs or information is discovered that could markedly shift the focus of the organization's efforts, it must be dealt with swiftly and not only at the end of a potentially long process.

Similarly, the feedback must be free-flowing, with all parts of the unit having constructive discussions about the intelligence process, from the leadership to those in the field using the end products. Just like most other business cycles, the goal is to reduce the time from discovery to implementation to reduce gaps in understanding the environment or to quickly mitigate capability shortfalls.

To ensure our hypothetical missile defense organization fully embraced all of the intelligence products, you directed evaluations and drills to compare unit responses to simulated enemy indicators. If any discrepancies or problems are observed, you may determine that the reports need to be revised or that new operating procedures are needed to better integrate the intelligence findings.

Applicability to Business

You likely already have some ideas on how you could apply this military intelligence process to areas in your organization like product development, marketing or developing strategies for competition with others offering similar products. While you're likely already familiar with business concepts like these, cybersecurity is another key part of your business that would benefit from your active involvement. Rather than just trusting cybersecurity to someone else in your organization, you could use a process like this to take an active role in prioritizing cybersecurity to protect your organization's precious financial and sensitive data resources. Furthermore, this process could be used to help improve the cybersecurity of your friends and family by raising your awareness in everything you do on computers or connected devices.

A few organizations may have enough resources to dedicate a team of analysts to collecting information, analyzing it and preparing reports that can be used by your IT department's engineers and system administrators. But most small businesses or organizations don't even have enough IT personnel to keep up with even the most basic daily activities, so of course they can't allocate more time to a complex cybersecurity intelligence gathering process.

However, just as military leaders from non-intelligence backgrounds can use the above process to help achieve their operational mission, you can achieve similar results using a process that has been modified to improve organizational cybersecurity awareness, whether the organization has an IT staff or not. In the next chapter, we'll explore a process designed to help improve any organization's cybersecurity by ensuring all personnel understand the risks and establishing mechanisms to improve their ability to help defend the castle.

CHAPTER 6

The Cybersecurity Awareness Process

Adapting the Intelligence Process

Let's review before proceeding. You followed Sun Tzu's advice and got to "Know The Enemy" in Chapter 3, but we only scratched the surface of the hacking techniques used and vulnerabilities exploited. Recalling that vulnerabilities are gradually fixed while new ones continue to be discovered, trying to be completely invulnerable to attack has so far proven to be impossible for most if not all organizations. Using this information as motivation, you got to "Know Yourself" in Chapter 4 as you defined your organization's mission, walked the castle walls to locate your treasures, inventoried devices, explored how everything was connected, and considered the security roles of your staff. And in Chapter 5, you learned how military commanders from various career fields use the DoD's intelligence process to reduce vulnerabilities against existing and emerging enemy threats to their mission. It should now be crystal clear that simply "knowing" a little about the enemy or relying on perhaps a dated view of your organization's IT infrastructure isn't enough; you need to be able to adjust your priorities and adapt your infrastructure to protect your treasure from the constant barrage of attacks made possible by known and unknown threats.

Security postures like *zero trust* and network infrastructures designed to *fail gracefully* have been developed to cope with the current threat reality, and perhaps your organization is exploring or already implementing these concepts. These are valuable technical implementations that will help improve security, but they won't bring *you* any closer to the decision-making process that could protect your organization when cybersecurity tools fail. Since military commanders from non-intelligence backgrounds are able to guide the military intelligence process to support their unit's mission, it stands to reason that your involvement in a similar process for cybersecurity is not only possible but could ensure that your organization's mission-critical digital treasures are secured at a level that matches your unique priorities.

In this chapter, we will review a version of the military intelligence process that has been modified to help non-IT leaders collect and understand information that can be used to protect organizations from cyber threats. Rather than focusing on intelligence gathering tasks that support operational military units, this Cybersecurity Awareness Process will help decision makers like you understand how cybersecurity can threaten businesses and organizations of any size. It will help you identify areas where operations and management practices can help protect your organization's important data. And most importantly, using this process will make you better informed for decisions on cybersecurity issues that you may have been reluctant to make or deferred to others because you weren't comfortable doing so. You are still the commander (or boss) of your organization, and this process can help you take ownership of cybersecurity.

Mission-Supporting Treasures

Recall that the unit's *Mission* was at the center of the DoD's Intelligence Process. In the Cybersecurity Awareness Process shown below, the center is labeled *Mission-Supporting Treasures*. These are the assets you defined in Chapter 4 that your organization would either struggle to operate without or would suffer in varying degrees should access to them be denied or lost. The focus of the process will remain on the Mission-Supporting Treasures at the center, which means the process will consist of collecting information about the threats to these treasures and assessing the effectiveness of your organization's resulting efforts to protect them. To do so effectively, you must have a strong understanding of the relative importance of each of these treasures; recall that some treasures may augment your organization's effectiveness while others are absolutely essential to the organization's survival.

Figure 2. The Cybersecurity Awareness Process
(© 2018, Samuel D. Bass)

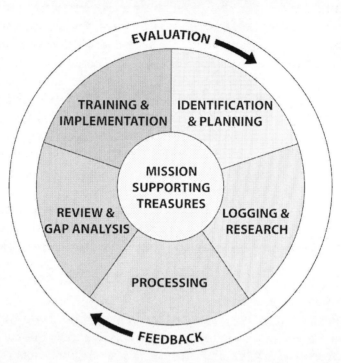

As we review this process in the next few sections, consider how you might apply it to your own organization and note the consistent differentiation between threats to *the organization* and just simply *the data.* That is intentional to emphasize that this process is protecting the mission-supporting treasures essential to the organization rather than simply ensuring your computers continue working like basic office equipment.

Identification and Planning

We will begin with the Identification and Planning phase, which is where you will set and guide your organization's cyber intelligence gathering efforts to ensure the central mission-supporting treasures are protected. *Identification* refers to finding new vulnerabilities, threats or attackers, and *Planning* refers to the steps you will take to either collect more information or strengthen your organization's defenses against them.

If your organization doesn't have a firm understanding of its infrastructure, the first time through this process will be somewhat time consuming as you'll focus more on system identification and vulnerability assessment. For example, you must know all of the IT systems in use at your organization and understand the vulnerabilities present on each of these systems. This includes understanding the current version of operating systems and software packages running on all devices, the status of all updates and patches, the connectivity requirements for wired and wireless devices, and the personnel entrusted to maintain these systems.

For more mature organizations, there may already be robust infrastructure management processes and network security systems in place. The IT department may utilize configuration management tools to manage software patches and updates or other security appliances to log network activity. In this case, identification may be the result of these systems reporting indications of new vulnerabilities or attacks.

Finally, all organizations must be responsive to external notifications like news articles, vendor alerts, and system updates as each can drive you to this phase of the Cybersecurity Awareness Process. For example, if a software vendor issues a security alert, you will enter this phase to identify which devices are vulnerable and need to be patched or updated.

Another crucial part of identification is that of determining who to consider an actual or potential enemy. In the missile defense scenario used in the last chapter, we had a clearly-defined enemy driving the commander's intelligence needs. Knowing exactly who the cyber enemy might be is impossible for most organizations because attacks regularly come from all around the world. We learned about hackers and the on-going cyber war in chapters 2 and 3, and I encouraged you to read one of the many free cyber threat reports available on line. Using information about the attacks in these reports, we can reasonably assume that most small organizations won't be the target of foreign government-sponsored hackers. Similarly, small businesses probably won't be targeted for industrial espionage purposes unless one has invented some valuable new technology, operates in a targeted industry, or does direct or indirect business with a government organization. Therefore, the most likely enemies are lone wolf hackers or hacking groups seeking notoriety or financial gain. You may identify more specific potential enemies for your own organization, but in general we must assume that anyone can be a cyber enemy of most organizations.

Unfortunately, these potential enemies include those inside your own organization. Recall that most cyber threat reports estimate that approximately 15% of all attacks were conducted or enabled by insiders. Current and former employees, happy and disgruntled, may have access to your mission-supporting treasure to varying degrees. As you go through the Identification and Planning phase, consider where you may be vulnerable to a sudden departure or change in behavior from one of your employees. Even a sudden illness or family emergency may make someone unavailable. If only one person has the password to a server or knows how to access certain features, their absence could slow or stop certain operations. Be sure to identify any personnel who might be "single points of failure" in your operations. While you may not identify everything in the first iteration of this process, the cyclical design allows you to enter any phase as new information is learned.

As you accomplish more of the Identification portion, the focus shifts to Planning. Similar to the Military Intelligence Process's Planning and Direction phase, which focused on organizing resources to collect information for an area of interest, Planning in this Cybersecurity Awareness Process may involve organizing personnel to conduct research or selecting security logging and auditing tools to look for attack indicators. You can use this phase to 'steer' your organization's cybersecurity posture based on the threats, vulnerabilities, and importance of protecting your organizational treasures.

Logging and Research

Similar to the DoD's Collection phase, the Logging and Research phase is where we collect information about the devices that store or process the organization's mission-supporting treasures. Logging refers to the process of recording network events on computers and network devices. Typical logging activities may include recording computer log-on or connection attempts, network accesses, file modifications, uploads and downloads, and system management changes. While some companies may be large enough to implement thorough logging processes or have robust network intrusion detection and scanning capabilities, most small businesses probably don't have any logging or auditing capabilities. This isn't unusual because most small businesses wouldn't think to install these kinds of devices without already having been a victim of an attack, unless they operate in an industry that mandates such security measures.

For those organizations that don't have the resources to conduct logging, the Research portion will enhance your understanding of vulnerabilities in existing systems and infrastructure to help improve the organization's security posture. In this phase, this research may include reviewing published vulnerability reports, reading cybersecurity alerts and news articles, or reviewing information about any current or prospective online service providers.

Processing

In this phase of the Cybersecurity Awareness Process, the raw data collected during the Logging and Research phase is converted into a form that can be used to either improve your security architecture or modify the procedures used throughout the organization. One example might be analyzing network activity logs for suspicious log-on attempts, unexpected or unusually large file transfers, or repeated external scanning of your network. Some of this processing may be conducted by automated log analysis or vulnerability assessment tools that come with various security appliances or services.

Another form of processing may be looking at inbound and outbound email traffic for signs of phishing or spearphishing attacks, or reviewing emails containing large attachments or sensitive data found with key word searches. The processing must be scheduled and recurring to ensure your network security is responding to current threats.

For organizations not yet logging any data, processing may not be needed unless you acquired data from a third-party vendor in the previous phase. However, there may be an opportunity for processing by standardizing any research collected in the previous phase. The goal of the processing phase is to make any collected information easier to understand and manage.

Review and Gap Analysis

In the Analysis and Production phase of the original Military Intelligence Process, reports were created to fulfill the mission commander's needs for training, changes to operational procedures, or justification for procuring additional resources or new capabilities. In the Cybersecurity Awareness Process, the Review and Gap Analysis phase is where the organization can identify where cyber security measures are not adequately aligned with the importance of the mission-supporting treasures. For example, if you learn that your highest-prioritized mission-supporting treasure has no access controls limiting who can change or delete that data, you would likely want to immediately review options for correcting that vulnerability.

Time spent in this phase of the process may result in solutions that could be implemented in the following phase, or it may uncover an information shortfall driving you to re-start the process at the Identification and Planning phase. This is therefore one of the most important phases of the

Cybersecurity Awareness Process. Without spending adequate time in this phase, the organization will be unable to adequately prioritize any cyber security improvement initiatives or projects. These decisions are truly risk management decisions, but focus on mitigating risks that threaten the organization's survival.

If this process identifies vulnerabilities to data that is not critical enough to have been prioritized over other mission-supporting treasures, perhaps the risk of exposure is acceptable. However, if there is some risk to mission-supporting data, the organizational leadership must be able to make a well-informed decision. For that reason, your involvement in these risk management decisions shouldn't be deferred to a potentially under-resourced department.

Training and Implementation

Once a cybersecurity shortfall is identified, changes will be applied in the Training and Implementation phase. Training is listed first because it is the human in the loop who regularly makes mistakes or takes shortcuts that are the first to be exploited by hackers. Additionally, a strong training program will help instill that healthy sense of cybersecurity paranoia in all levels of the organization that could guide future decisions influencing the protection of the company's mission-supporting treasures. Training in this phase might include any new cybersecurity tools or procedures implemented to address the previously identified gaps, but also awareness training to help users identify new attacks against the organization.

If a new security threat is deemed sufficient enough to warrant new security devices or procedures, the Implementation portion of this phase is where these improvements are initiated and monitored. For example, if you noted a spike in a specific kind of phishing email in the Identification phase, the Implementation portion of this phase is where changes to the email filters may be made or a new email security system is purchased and installed.

Evaluation and Feedback

As your organization conducts its business, continually assess your team's cybersecurity awareness and the security of your mission-supporting treasures. As you use this process on a regular basis, you will learn more about cybersecurity threats, vulnerabilities and best practices, and you should see continual improvements in your security. If you don't see improvements, grow more concerned about your growing list of vulnerabilities, or worse yet fall victim to an attack, spend more time on this process and focus your efforts. Since Evaluation and Feedback encompass all phases of the process, you can jump in to any phase as needed.

Consider the Cybersecurity Awareness Process as a guide, just as common sense is your guide when considering physical security. When moving to a new location, you are selective about who has spare keys to your home or office, you might buy better locks, install security cameras, or use motion-activated lights. You are in essence following the same process in that you are identifying threats, analyzing vulnerabilities, and implementing new security measures. But for most organizations, cybersecurity may seem like invisible and mysterious territory. While cyberspace might be considered a tough neighborhood, you can use this process to guide your learning and decision making to protect your mission critical treasures. In the next chapter, we will walk through the process to improve the cybersecurity of a typical small business.

CHAPTER 7

Case Study - Applying the Cybersecurity Awareness Process

A Typical Organization

Imagine you're the owner of a small graphics design business that specializes in creating advertisements for local print magazines. You have a dozen computers in your office that support 15 graphic designers, sales representatives and administrative assistants, but you don't have any on-site IT support personnel. Some of your team members are fairly knowledgeable about computers, but only in the consumer sense of regularly using their own computers and devices and correcting minor problems. The rest know only the basics of using a computer and aren't adept at troubleshooting problems. Let's imagine that half of your computers are about five years old, and the other half were purchased less than a year ago. You also have several company-owned tablets and smartphones for key staff members. Your office has a commercial internet connection through a cable television provider, which connects your computers and other devices via wired and wifi network connections. Since cellphone signal coverage is poor in the building, you allowed your employees to connect their personal devices to the office's wifi network. You have a few large-format network printers and a network storage device for storing and sharing large data files. Suppose that you hired a local web developer to create a public web page for displaying samples of your work and your business contact information, and your email accounts are hosted on a commercial email vendor but using your own company's domain name. You recently used the "Know Yourself" chapter to collect detailed information about all of the above devices and services, and we'll use that information as we apply the Cybersecurity Awareness Process.

Mission-Supporting Treasures

Using the Know Yourself chapter on this hypothetical graphic design business, you identify the following mission-supporting treasures in prioritized order:

1. Customer contact and billing database
2. Historical artwork files
3. Email archives
4. Annual license keys for creative suite software applications
5. Web page content

You might place different priorities on these items but consider that repeat customers are essential and giving competitors access to both of the first two priorities could be devastating to a graphic design business. The same could be said for your email archives as they could reveal details about pricing deals and concepts that competitors could use to their advantage. Lost license keys to software suites could be re-purchased, and any temporary loss or defacement of your web page could be quickly replaced but would still cost you time, money and perhaps some embarrassment.

Use similar logic when you prioritize the treasures for your own organization but realize certain priorities may be more important during certain parts of the year or change entirely from year to year. This Cybersecurity Awareness Process will be flexible and responsive to your needs, so be sure to consider changes to your mission-supporting treasures or how you might re-prioritize them every time you use this process.

Identification and Planning

You completed the inventory while walking the castle walls as guided in the Know Yourself chapter, but let's dig a little deeper into the vulnerabilities that might be present on your business's computers, tablets and smartphones.

Table 3. Sample Inventory

Partial List of Devices	Age	Operating System
Three (3) desktop computers	8 mos	Windows 10, Version 1709
Three (3) laptop computers	5 yrs	Windows 7, Service Pack 1
Three (3) desktop computers	6 mos	MacOS High Sierra, Version 10.13.3
Three (3) laptop computers	5 yrs	MacOS El Capitan, Version 10.11.6
One (1) 10" iPad tablet	1 yr	iOS 11.3
One (1) 8" Android tablet	2 yrs	Android 7.0 Nougat
Two (2) iPhone 7 phones	1 yr	iOS 11.3
One (1) Samsung Galaxy S6 phone	2 yrs	Android 6.0 Marshmallow
One (1) Android phone	4 mos	Android 8.1 Oreo

(Note: all brands and versions are used in this chapter only as examples; no endorsements or critiques implied. Product names are the registered trademarks of their respective owners.)

Notice that your hypothetical business has *eight* different operating systems on the devices that are connected to your treasures. This means you need to research eight different platforms because each version of an operating system has different code and thus different vulnerabilities. But simply searching for threats against each operating system version isn't enough; recall that during the recommended inventory process you should have reviewed the additional software packages installed on all of these devices. Your business uses Adobe Photoshop and Illustrator, numerous photo manipulation tools, office productivity tools from Microsoft and Apple, and dozens of apps on the tablets and smartphones. Don't forget the other devices seen while walking the castle, like your printers, network storage device, wifi router and the software on your business's public web page or email provider. Your to-do list for threat research has quickly grown to dozens of different software packages and operating systems on a range of devices.

There are other areas you could explore in this Identification and Planning phase, but already there is a lot of research to conduct. You decide to address other areas like <u>Identifying</u> potential enemies or threats for the next iteration through this process. Instead, you begin by making a Plan to tackle this long list you have assembled.

The list of devices and software packages is long enough that it would take too much time for one person to adequately research alone. Since this small business doesn't have an IT support staff, you might think it's time to look outside the organization for assistance. However, this is a perfect opportunity to help instill in your organization that healthy sense of paranoia we discussed in chapter 4.

You decide that one of the first cybersecurity training sessions for your team will be reviewing this list together and tasking each person to conduct some basic research on vulnerabilities. Since your list has about thirty devices, operating systems and software packages, each person on your team will be able to research just two or three items in a relatively short time. By searching and collecting vulnerability information for their assigned items on your list, each member of your organization will learn the seriousness of the threats in the ongoing cyber war. And most importantly, everyone in your organization will become better "castle wall lookouts" in this cyber war.

Logging and Research

Since you don't have any devices Logging network activity, you decide to conduct your Research during a "Cybersecurity Awareness Day" and as planned, you assign each person on the team two or three of the items from your list. The US government funds various cybersecurity programs and organizations that provide numerous excellent resources. One of the best resources you can use at no charge is the Common Vulnerabilities and Exposures (CVE) List that consolidates and standardizes vulnerability reports for hardware and software. My recommendation is to have your team use the "advanced search" option on the National Vulnerability Database (NVD) hosted by the Department of Commerce's National Institute for Standards Technology (NIST) website.[12] For those not comfortable with the options presented on the NVD site, have them start with the CVE database[13] published by MITRE for the U.S. Department of Homeland Security's US-CERT office of Cybersecurity and Communications. The NVD site uses the same standardized CVE

---

[12] https://nvd.nist.gov/vuln/search

[13] http://cve.mitre.org/cve/search_cve_list.html

database hosted on MITRE's site, but the more advanced search options on the NVD site usually make it a better option.

Using a search term like "Windows 10," "Adobe Photoshop 18.1," or "iOS 11.3" on these sites should result in a list of several (or numerous) vulnerabilities.[14] Some searches will result in more entries than others, and some will say the vulnerability exists only in versions *prior* to the version number used in the search. If some searches return zero results or too many non-applicable results, have your team discuss their individual search methods and successes when using different keyword combinations or advanced search options. As your team conducts their searches, have them either take screen shots of the results or copy the results and paste them into a spreadsheet. The key is to learn as a group and have everyone see first-hand how old versions of software can leave the organization vulnerable if not updated.

For those on your team tasked with researching hardware, the NIST's NVD site is an excellent resource for searching products by vendor name. Utilize the advanced search option and fill in the vendor and product information in the Common Platform Enumerations (CPE) section. Your team members may be overwhelmed by the breadth of CPE options, but learning by trial and error will be time well spent. When looking for vulnerabilities for a device like a printer or router, focus on the *firmware*[15] version on these devices themselves. Your team will likely have to research how to determine the current firmware version number for each device, but this knowledge will help later when implementing fixes. You may also have some applications installed on your computers to manage devices like scanners and storage devices; be sure to research vulnerabilities for these software packages as well. The following table shows how your hypothetical team researched vulnerabilities on a few of the inventoried devices and software packages.

---

[14] Try searching for "Adobe Photoshop 18.1" on both databases and compare the results to see how the same search term may result in different lists. Some results might not apply to the version you are actually using, so try using a more refined search to reduce extraneous findings.

[15] You probably know that hardware is the physical device like a computer, printer or handheld device. Similarly, software is the code that runs on these devices that can be modified or changed over time by the user. Think of *firmware* as the code between these two layers that is required to make the hardware function. Some device firmware can be updated to address security and performance issues, so learning how to keep this firmware updated is critical.

Table 4. Sample Research Findings

Type	Details	Search Method and Terms
Desktop OS	Windows 10 (Build 1511)	NVD CPE with Vendor = microsoft, Product = Windows 10, Version = 10:1511
Mobile OS	Apple iOS 11.3	NVD CPE search not helpful because version wasn't listed Then searched "iOS 11.3" on both NVD and CVE
Mobile OS	Android 8.1	NVD CPE with Vendor = google, Product = android, Version = 8.1
Mobile OS	Android 6.0	NVD CPE with Vendor = google, Product = android, Version = 6.0
Mobile OS	Samsung Galaxy S6	NVD CPE with Vendor = samsung, Product = galaxy_s6, Version left blank
WiFi Router Firmware	Apple Airport Extreme (Version 5.5)	NVD CPE with Vendor = apple, Product = airport_extreme_base_station_firmware, Version = 5.5
Printer Firmware	Lexmark Firmware (Version ATL 02.048)	NVD CPE with Vendor = lexmark, Product = printer_firmware, Version = atl.02.048
Software	Adobe Photoshop (Version 18.1.0)	NVD CPE with Vendor = adobe, Product = photoshop, Version = 18.1.0 Then searched "adobe photoshop 18.1" on both NVD and CPE
Software	Microsoft Word for Windows (Version 16.0.4266)	NVD CPE with Vendor = microsoft, Product = word, Version = 2016 Because exact version wasn't listed, searched "microsoft word 16" on both NVD and CPE

You direct your team to search for vulnerabilities in all of their assigned devices, operating systems and software packages, then record the results in a spreadsheet template you shared beforehand. If any device or software package has no entries, you will try together as a team on both web sites to ensure the research was conducted with the best search options. During this phase, you ensure everyone participates to maximize learning. The volume of vulnerabilities your team discovers should catch everyone's attention about the security of devices in the office and in their homes.

Processing

Since your hypothetical business wasn't logging any network activity yet, there isn't any processing required on the list of vulnerabilities that your team collected. For your first time through this process however, you will use this Processing phase to ensure that all of the data is in a master spreadsheet and is organized well enough to make later updates easier. A sample spreadsheet showing the compiled results of your team's research is shown below:

Table 5. Sample Processed Findings

Name	Product	Vulnerability ID	Summary	CVSS Severity
Alice	Windows 10	CVE-2018-0942	Internet Explorer in Microsoft Windows 7 SP1, Windows Server 2008 SP2 and R2 SP1, Windows 8.1 and Windows RT 8.1, Windows Server 2012 and R2, Windows 10 Gold, 1511, 1607, 1703, 1709, and Windows Server 2016 allow elevation of privilege, due to how Internet Explorer handles zone and integrity settings, aka "Internet Explorer Elevation of Privilege Vulnerability".	V3: 2.6 LOW
Bob	Windows 10	CVE-2018-0935	Internet Explorer in Microsoft Windows 7 SP1, Windows Server 2008 and R2 SP1, Windows 8.1 and Windows RT 8.1, Windows Server 2012 and R2, Windows 10 Gold, 1511, 1607, 1703, 1709, and Windows Server 2016 allows remote code execution, due to how the scripting engine handles objects in memory, aka "Scripting Engine Memory Corruption Vulnerability". This CVE ID is unique from CVE-2018-0876, CVE-2018-0889, CVE-2018-0893, and CVE-2018-0925.	V3: 7.5 HIGH
Carol	Photoshop 18.1	CVE-2017-11304	An issue was discovered in Adobe Photoshop 18.1.1 (2017.1.1) and earlier versions. An exploitable use-after-free vulnerability exists. Successful exploitation could lead to arbitrary code execution.	V3: 9.8 CRITICAL
Dean	Photoshop 18.1	CVE-2017-11303	An issue was discovered in Adobe Photoshop 18.1.1 (2017.1.1) and earlier versions. An exploitable memory corruption vulnerability exists. Successful exploitation could lead to arbitrary code execution.	V3: 9.8 CRITICAL

(Note: The data in this table was researched at the time of writing and is subject to change. For demonstration purposes only.)

Reviewing each column, you will see listed the name of the person on your team who did the search, what product they searched, the resulting Vulnerability ID code to make future reference easier, a summary of the vulnerability, and the relative severity. By maintaining a master spreadsheet, you will be able to delete items as they are patched or updated on all of your devices or referred to later if there are concerns about processing your treasures on a particular device or software package.

You may be concerned by the technical details listed on the table, but for the purposes of this time through the process it is enough to only read the Summary and the Severity to get a general feel for the potential threat to your treasures. In particular, focus your attention on the affected versions and the severity. We will learn how to review the processed data in the next phase of the process.

Review and Gap Analysis

Once you collect everyone's inputs, you will <u>Review</u> the list of systems and software and the even longer list of vulnerabilities for each of these systems in use at our business. One of the first things you noticed in the Identification phase was the variety of operating systems and varying ages of the installed versions. In the Research phase, your team noted the number of vulnerabilities for older systems and software was generally higher than the number found in newer systems and software versions.

Looking at Table 5, both Alice and Bob's searches on Windows 10 describe in the vulnerability summary that versions "1511, 1607, 1703, and 1709" were susceptible to two different attacks. From Table 3 earlier in this chapter, notice that your office's computers are all running build number 1511. Therefore, upgrading from the old software to the newest version (1803 at the time of publication) would immediately eliminate some vulnerabilities. Unfortunately, some devices may not be capable of being updated to the newest operating system, and some of your business's crucial software tools might not work on newer operating systems due to their age or vendor restrictions.

In this phase, your team determined that the software packages and firmware could be updated on all devices except for two items on your list:

- One laptop must be kept on Windows 7 because a legacy piece of graphics design software won't run on Windows 10
- The 8" Android tablet doesn't have an operating system update available, so it has to remain on Android 7.0 Nougat

Knowing that these two devices will continue to have un-corrected vulnerabilities force you to make some risk management decisions. Since the legacy graphics design software won't be updated by the vendor, you need to decide whether to procure a new software package or to continue using a vulnerable platform. And because the tablet can't be updated to the latest operating system, you need to determine whether to replace it with a newer model or somehow restrict what company treasures are processed on the tablet. These are all cost and risk management decisions that might drive training costs and possibly short-term productivity losses, but you must make these decisions in the context of protecting your mission-supporting treasures.

Training and Implementation

For your graphic design business, the very act of going through this process together for the first time is a great form of <u>Training</u>. Examples of later training sessions include any new policies you put in place to improve network security, training on how to identify phishing and spearphishing attacks using actual messages your business received, or discussions about a news report or a new software vulnerability bulletin.

In the Review and Gap Analysis phase, you came up with a long list of fixes to implement in your business. Your team identified the need for numerous software updates and you made decisions about the two devices that couldn't be updated. Most operating systems and software packages automatically receive update notifications, but usually some user action is required. In both cases an administrator account may be needed to perform system and software updates. Depending on your organization, it may be a time-consuming process if only one user has an administrator account on your computers. The <u>Implementation</u> phase may take some time to complete, so remember to request feedback and evaluate this phase like you should on all other phases. Be careful not to take shortcuts like sharing administrator accounts or other time-saving ideas. Use your favorite search tool to research any idea before trying it as you may open your organization to more vulnerabilities than you wanted. You will likely find many examples of how a cybersecurity shortcut caused more problems than they might be worth.

Next, you have to implement your decisions for the laptop and tablet that can't be updated. Let's assume that the legacy software on the laptop is used to show clients various modifications to photographs while out of your office. The legacy software package requires that the photographs are stored on the laptop, but once they are on the hard drive, no other connectivity is required. A potential replacement software package costs several hundred dollars and will require some user training. You decide to defer that cost and effort but will reduce the risks posed by the older operating system by eliminating all web access and removing all other software packages that were configured to access your mission-supporting treasures. To get the photographs on the computer while limiting exposure to external threats, you are considering using an external hard drive, optical media like DVDs, or allowing the staff to connect the laptop to the office network only long enough to copy the photographs. Based on team input, the estimated costs of an external hard drive or optical media, and the potential risks posed by each solution, you decide that using DVDs to transfer images to the laptop and then keeping those DVDs for archival backups is the cheapest, safest and most useful alternative.

Finally, you decide to use the old tablet only as an "internet reader." In this capacity, it will only be used in the office to show clients your public web page or for casual browsing by employees on breaks. All email clients and other software applications will be removed so the tablet can't be used for business email or processing any of the company's treasures.

As you conclude this phase of the process, you take the opportunity to train your staff about these new restrictions and ensure they understand the risks and consequences of not complying with your policies. You demonstrate how to create and label the transfer and backup DVDs to ensure that all users aren't tempted to take any shortcuts around your new security procedures. It is likely that during training, potential good ideas will come from your staff, so be sure to keep this in mind for the next Evaluation and Feedback portion of the process.

Evaluation and Feedback

Now that you made a sizable number of changes to the devices on your list, you should endeavor to keep your inventory updated and watch for updates to software and firmware. Now that you understand the software and operating systems in use, you can quickly assess news about cybersecurity events and inject that information into any phase of the process. Additionally, your team should feel empowered to bring other concerns to your attention at any time. This is particularly true if you implementing a change and note during the course of business a secondary concern or unintended consequence arises. It is important that feedback flows freely so that an evaluation can be made about the security of your mission-supporting treasures. Without this mechanism, organizations may lose focus and allow convenience to compromise security.

A Cyclical Process

You completed one iteration of this process, but there are still some significant items that need to be addressed from the initial Identification phase of this scenario to protect your mission-supporting treasures. If we continued our review of this scenario, we would start the process again by considering the cybersecurity of our public web page and cloud-based email solutions. You were concerned because you didn't have a firm understanding of who had access to what systems, nor did you know what could be done if one of those people unexpectedly became unavailable. Because the subject of managing sensitive user accounts and passwords might be contentious to those who might fear losing administrator access or those thinking they should be given access, this probably shouldn't involve the entire team. This is a sensitive risk management and personnel management issue, so you should limit participation in this particular iteration of the process to those you trust implicitly.

Follow the same process starting with Identification and Planning to determine who has the master user accounts and passwords for these services or systems, Research specifics about the provider and any software packages in use, and then determine what Gaps may exist should anyone identified as a single point of failure become suddenly unavailable. You may decide that for your next Training and Implementation phase you need to change account passwords, create additional administrator accounts, and train others on any new responsibilities you may delegate.

As you learn more about your organization's IT infrastructure and cybersecurity posture, your decision-making process will become quicker and more focused on protecting your organization. Every time you go through this process, your cybersecurity posture should improve and your users should be better trained to help protect your castle and its mission-supporting treasures.

CHAPTER 8
Conclusion

Trust No One? Really?

By now, you should have gained both a sense of cybersecurity awareness and healthy paranoia by heeding Sun Tzu's advice to better know both your organization and what the enemy is capable of doing. While chasing hackers and delving into your organization's IT infrastructure may not be in your domain of expertise, the stewardship of your organization's treasures is likely your responsibility. At the same time, if you truly Trust No One and try to do too much by yourself, then you won't be very effective as a leader. That is where the previously discussed adage of "trust but verify" is most applicable. You need to achieve enough comfort with the subject of cybersecurity so that you can trust your team, but you are able to verify that the very basics are being applied to protect your treasures.

Sun Tzu understood that a general's expertise in various disciplines like logistics, finances and planning was essential to victory in war. Being a successful leader in a modern organization normally requires a breadth of competence in similar business skills. In your organization, you are likely expected to responsibly manage assigned resources, control expenses, protect resources from theft or abuse, and lead those in your chain of command to ensure mission success. You may have honed your leadership skills while playing team sports in school, added some occupational or technical skills in college, and developed operational skills through years of hands-on experience. And now that you know your organization's survival relies on protecting your mission-supporting treasures from cyber attacks, it should be clear that you are responsible for another task: enhancing your organization's cybersecurity awareness.

As you've learned in this book, you don't need to know how to configure a firewall or install an advanced email scanning tool. Nor do you need to be able to pick specific cyber countermeasures for deployment or have a thorough understanding of your system architectures. But you must be able to identify threat sources and understand the risks posed by connected systems and be able to assess the potential impact of both on your business. By using the information in this book, you can now determine what your mission-supporting treasures are, develop a general understanding of whether you're adequately protecting those treasures or not, and can identify some common-sense changes that your organization can make to immediately improve your cybersecurity to keep those treasures safe. And most importantly, you should know when you need to ask for outside help in accomplishing any of these tasks.

Next Steps

If while reading this book you didn't take the time to define your mission and mission-supporting treasures, you should accomplish that as soon as you finish reading this final chapter. Use Chapter 4, Know Yourself, and Appendix 1 as references. Once you have a solid understanding of what you need to protect, use the Cybersecurity Awareness Process to gain a better understanding of how your treasures are protected. Appendix 1 lists the Key Actions and Desired Results that most organizations would find applicable for each phase. Use the additional resources listed in the other appendices to help you make incremental improvements to reduce the risks facing your mission-supporting treasures. Continue using this process to identify other treasures, determine their relative prioritization, strengthen security, and eliminate weaknesses in your cyber castle.

Remember that the first few times through the process will be more focused on *knowing yourself* as you will inventory equipment, learn where information is stored and processed, and more importantly discover how (or even if) your treasures are protected. Remember to involve your team and take every opportunity to research and learn that which you don't understand. If there is too much to research alone, break the work up into smaller tasks. Share research projects amongst your team, split up the inventorying process with a trusted partner, and make a habit of using the Cybersecurity Awareness Process. Every adjustment you make over time will improve your cyber security.

The cyclical nature of the Cybersecurity Awareness Process means precisely that: it is a never-ending cycle of reducing vulnerabilities and improving awareness to counter the continuously evolving risks. You will become comfortable with this process the more you follow it, just as military commanders from non-intelligence backgrounds grow comfortable setting priorities for their intelligence professionals to help accomplish the mission. And similar to how military commanders reach the end of their capabilities in certain situations without additional resources, you will likely find a point where you need outside help. This will be the point where you will need to make a risk management and business continuity decision. You may have to spend money by procuring new services or equipment, hiring additional IT staff members, or purchasing some form of cyber insurance. But now that you have more information about the situation, you will be in the position to make a well-informed decision for your organization's unique mission and cybersecurity priorities.

Use the Cybersecurity Awareness Process as you explore these options so that you take the appropriate steps in the planning, research and analysis for this important decision. The process will help you ensure that whatever solution you decide to implement properly addresses the risks to your treasures. If you determine the best course of action is to enlist a professional consultant, seek the services of a certified cybersecurity expert known for their work in both the region and the sector in which you operate. You can use the cumulative results of the Cybersecurity Awareness Process to educate any third-party experts who may be entrusted with key details of your organization and mission-supporting treasures, but ensure proper legal protections like non-disclosure agreements are in place. Remember at all times to consider how any actions will affect your treasures, particularly when new personnel are introduced to those treasures.

As your organization's cybersecurity posture matures and you explore solutions to reduce risks, you'll discover numerous sources of proven cybersecurity policies, procedures and standards of behavior for those administering IT systems. You'll find recommended improvements such as establishing user accountability by logging all IT system activities, preventing fraud by implementing separation of duties in sensitive business processes, and ensuring business continuity by establishing backup and restoration plans. Processes like these can be found in more detailed books or may be suggested by consultants but scoping any solution to your organization and your budget will of course be your responsibility. Consult Appendix 2 for links to several government-funded organizations that provide free guides of varying levels of detail on these same topics.

Until Then...

In Chapter 3, I suggested that it has taken about 250 years to develop relatively safe automobiles, yet that safety seems to be the result of automating our vehicles almost to the point of removing humans from behind the wheel.

Today, all of our computers and mobile devices are designed by humans, software is programmed by humans, networks are operated by humans, and billions of humans around the world use these devices. Yet a hacker exploiting a single human mistake can compromise a device, burrow into a network, destroy data or equipment, and potentially ruin an entire organization. This may mean we will be actively involved in cybersecurity until around 2050 when our connected devices might be fully self-configured and completely immune to compromises caused by the intentional or accidental acts of humans.

I really hope that estimate is wrong, but until that day comes, don't get comfortable with your organization's cybersecurity and **Trust No One**, because no one should care more about your data than you.

CHAPTER 9
Appendices

Appendix 1
The Cybersecurity Awareness Process

The following is not a checklist for this process, but rather a reference guide with recommendations for your own implementation. For each phase below, consider the various <u>Key Actions</u> and <u>Desired/Possible Results</u> to determine where you might focus your organization's efforts on each run through this process. Key Actions are some of the activities you should consider for each phase, and the Desired/Possible Results are what could result from those actions. Some of the Key Actions listed below may need to be fully implemented before you can accomplish other Key Actions in the same or following phase, and each of the Desired/Possible Results might come only after some or all actions are accomplished.

As you use this process to discover vulnerabilities and implement improvements, reference other guides and books specific to your type of organization. Using this process as you consider recommendations from other sources will ensure your efforts are focused on your organization's uniquely prioritized mission-supporting treasures. For the smallest organizations, keeping your systems updated and your users trained may be all that your available resources allow. For larger organizations, more advanced cybersecurity solutions and compliance tools are essential. Reference the sites listed in <u>Appendix 2, Useful Online Resources</u> for valuable but free advice for a variety of organizations and environments.

Mission-Supporting Treasures

Key Actions
- Identify treasures critical to the organization's continued operation
- Prioritize the treasures (and re-prioritize them as needed)

Desired Results
- Your organization's mission-supporting treasures are clearly identified and prioritized year-round according to your unique mission

Identification & Planning

Key Actions
- Identify where mission supporting treasures are stored or processed
- Identify all systems by make, model and operating system (to include firmware if applicable)
- Identify single points of failure (equipment and personnel)
- Identify the appearance of new system vulnerabilities, potential enemies or indications of probing or attack
- Plan research or event logging strategies for the next phase

Possible Results
- Detailed device, network and service provider inventories
- Lists of potential single points of failure (hardware, software or personnel)
- Plans for how to best conduct research on vulnerabilities, maintain inventories or monitor employee duties
- Plans for system logging and auditing

Logging & Research

Key Actions
- Activate logging on security devices
- Conduct research as planned in the previous phase

Possible Results
- Copies of downloaded security reports or bulletins
- Copies of applicable or industry-specific cybersecurity articles
- Detailed results of hardware and/or software vulnerability research
- Detailed contact details of key personnel or supporting service providers

Processing

Key Actions
- Activate log analysis systems or manually review logs
- Standardize, summarize or simplify the research collected in the previous phase

Possible Results
- Event log reports that highlight any potential threats to mission supporting treasures
- Easy to maintain rosters of equipment, service providers and key personnel
- Quality data for decision-maker review in the next phase

Review & Gap Analysis

Key Actions
- Review vulnerabilities and options for remediation
- Review unused, unneeded, or out-of-date hardware and software
- Identify mission-supporting treasures that are un-protected or under-protected; review options for protection
- Determine alternatives for any single points of failure

Possible Results
- Indications of a scan/attack that drive you to the Identification and Planning phase
- Decisions to replace, eliminate or limit the use of old hardware or software
- Decisions to improve resilience for any single points of failure
- Software updates are identified and validated for implementation

Training & Implementation

Key Actions
- Implement new security solutions or procedures
- Update all systems, software and firmware
- Replace or remove vulnerable equipment or limit its use
- Replace or remove vulnerable software or limit its use
- Implement data backup and encryption
- Train users on new duties, security solutions or procedures
- Train users on common and emerging threats

Possible Results
- All software, operating systems and equipment firmware is updated
- Risky hardware and software has reduced access to mission supporting treasures
- Mission-supporting treasures are encrypted, archived and better protected from loss or compromise
- Computer and/or network security tools are installed to protect the organization
- Users are well trained and understand organizational policies

Evaluation & Feedback
Key Actions
- Observe the overall cybersecurity posture
- Seek and provide cybersecurity-related feedback
- Identify the need to enter any phase of the process

Desired Results
- All personnel in your organization are aware of the risks, able to bring concerns to your attention, and help support all cybersecurity initiatives
- Your organization's mission-supporting treasures are better protected from current risks and your cybersecurity posture is flexible enough to react to emerging risks

Appendix 2
Useful Online Resources

The following collection of web sites will be useful to any organization. Some offer helpful guides, others detailed vulnerability and threat data from attacks being reported around the world. Another potential training session for your staff could be reviewing these sites together and determining which guides or lists of best practices can be implemented in your organization.

National Institute of Standards and Technology (NIST)
https://www.nist.gov/topics/cybersecurity

Originally created to help the United States compete with industrial powerhouse economies in Europe, the national laboratories that comprise NIST are now fully engaged in helping the US improve its cybersecurity. There are many resources and tools available on their website listed above, but I highly recommend reading the report titled Small Business Information Security: The Fundamentals, which can be found here:
http://nvlpubs.nist.gov/nistpubs/ir/2016/NIST.IR.7621r1.pdf

The Center for Internet Security (CIS) Critical Security Controls for Effective Cyber Defense
https://www.cisecurity.org/

The CIS is a non-profit entity that seeks to protect private and public organizations against cyber threats. The site linked above includes numerous guides and best practices to help secure systems and data against common attacks. Many of the products are available in multiple languages including Japanese.

United States Computer Emergency Readiness Team (US-CERT)
https://www.us-cert.gov

US-CERT plays in important role in our national cybersecurity by analyzing threats, responding to cyber incidents, and sharing cybersecurity information with similar agencies around the world. A great deal of useful information about threats, alerts and protection measures can be found on their website. US-CERT also has a useful checklist for reporting any cyber incident against your organization. Reporting an incident is voluntary for private organizations, but government entities must report cyber attacks to help other government agencies properly defend against future attacks. More information can be found here:
https://www.us-cert.gov/incident-notification-guidelines

National Initiative For Cybersecurity Education (NICE)
https://www.nist.gov/itl/applied-cybersecurity/national-initiative-cybersecurity-education-nice

Operated by the NIST, the NICE program's mission is to "is to energize and promote a robust network and an ecosystem of cybersecurity education, training, and workforce development." To accomplish that, NICE provides resources, guides and information about cybersecurity seminars and education.

The Small Business Administration (SBA)
https://www.sba.gov/managing-business/cybersecurity/

The SBA is a federal government agency tasked to help guide small businesses, encourage competition and help grow the national economy. Today, guiding small businesses in cybersecurity with free resources is an essential part of the SBA's mission.

MITRE CVE
http://cve.mitre.org/cve/search_cve_list.html

The Common Vulnerabilities and Exposures (CVE) site is hosted by the MITRE Corporation, a US non-profit company dedicated to US government research and development efforts. The CVE list is the authoritative source for publicly known cybersecurity vulnerabilities, and the CVE common identifiers (CVE IDs) used in this list are used around the world.

———

National Vulnerability Database (NVD)
https://web.nvd.nist.gov/view/vuln/search

The NVD is the U.S. government repository of vulnerability data hosted by the National Institute of Standards and Technology (NIST) Computer Security Division, Information Technology Laboratory and sponsored by the Department of Homeland Security's National Cyber Security Division. This database expands the information available about each vulnerability in the MITRE CVE database and is my recommended location for researching vulnerabilities in your organization while following the Cybersecurity Awareness Process.

Appendix 3
Resources for Friends and Family

The "OnGuard Online" (http://onguardonline.gov/) program offer tips and resources to help consumers guard against Internet fraud, secure their computers, and protect personal information, while "Stay Safe Online" (http://www.staysafeonline.org/) promotes safe behavior online.

————

The NetSmartz Workshop provides educational materials for children and teens that can be found at http://www.netsmartz.org/.

————

The "Stop. Think. Connect." campaign is aimed at the general public with the goal of educating everyone about cyber threats and improving on-line security for all. (http://www.dhs.gov/stopthinkconnect)

Appendix 4
Basic Cybersecurity Questions

Computers
How many servers?
How many desktop computers?
How many laptop computers?
What Operating Systems and Versions do we use?
How old are all computers?
Are all computers on an asset inventory?
Are computers regularly patched with the latest security updates? Who ensures this?
Are any computers too old to get updated, and if so, why are they on our network?
Are users able to install any application, drivers or extensions they want on our computers?

Smartphones, tablets and other connected/smart devices
How many smartphones and tablets?
How many connected or smart devices do we have? *(Ignore whether they are currently connected or not.)*
What Operating Systems and Versions?
How old are these devices?
Are these devices on an asset inventory?
Do we remotely update and manage mobile devices, or rely on vendor updates? Who ensures this?
Do we update the connected/smart devices? If so, who updates these devices?
Are any devices too old to get updated, and if so, why are they on our network?
Are users able to install any apps they want on these devices?

Basic Cybersecurity Questions (cont.)

Web or Cloud Services
What web services do we use (i.e., email, storage, collaboration)?
Who has billing and management accounts/passwords for these services?
Do we use third-party add-ons or drivers?
Do we perform network and user account logging and auditing?
Are employees trained to maintain physical control of devices?
Wired Network
How many computers are plugged in to the network?
Who has passwords to and manages the networking equipment?
Are any connected/smart devices like copiers, scanners, VTC systems, or other devices plugged in to the wired network?
Wifi Network
What encryption protocol is enabled?
Who was the wifi password for adding devices?
Are devices added whenever needed and without control, or is there a regulated process for adding new devices to the network to ensure security?
What devices are using the wifi network right now? Are any devices logging in after business hours?
Are any neighboring businesses in range of our wifi network?
Does the wifi network signal extend beyond the physical confines of your organization?

Appendix 5
Sample Mission-Supporting Treasures

Organization	Treasure
Any business	Cash in bank accounts, payroll accounts, etc.
Any business	Customer contact information
Any business	Customer billing information (account numbers or credit card numbers)
Any business	"Frequent Buyer Card" member database
Any business	Business plans or strategies
Any business	Public web page
Any business	Email system and email archives
Manufacturing business	Product designs, drawings or schematics
Construction company	Blueprints, plans, supplier contracts, etc.
Software Company	Computer source code
Photographer, Videographer or Media Company	Digital assets like videos, photographs, drawings and graphics
Bank or Investment Firm	Financial transaction histories
Law firm	Client lists, briefs, files, findings, etc.
Hospital or Doctor's office	HIPA files (digital health records, etc.)
Restaurant	Reservation systems, point of sale systems, recipes, menus, food vendor contracts, etc.
Professional musician	Recordings, sheet music, digital assets
News outlet (online, print, television)	Video or audio recordings, articles and web pages
Retail, Grocery or Convenience Store	Physical products being sold or serviced, inventory records, vendor contracts, etc.
Security Company	Remote monitoring systems, communications with field units
Online content provider	Digital assets and un-interrupted connectivity

Appendix 6
Cyber Threat Reports

The following reports were the result of several searches for "cyber threat report" in my preferred search engine. No endorsements implied in any of these reports, but I do recommend you conduct your own searches quarterly or at the absolute minimum annually. Some reports found via search may require registration via email, so please use the appropriate caution by ensuring the site's authenticity before sharing your name and email address. If you aren't convinced you need to try using the Cybersecurity Awareness Process in your organization, reading just one of the reports below will change your mind. Some of the following links may change without notice.

"Global Threat Intelligence Center (GTIC) Quarterly Threat Intelligence Report" By NTT Security (US)
https://www.nttsecurity.com/en-us/gtic-2017-q3-threat-intelligence-report

"2018 Internet Security Threat Report" by Symantec
https://www.symantec.com/security-center/threat-report

"McAfee Labs Quarterly Threat Report" By McAfee
https://www.mcafee.com/us/resources/reports/rp-quarterly-threats-jun-2017.pdf

"Annual or Midyear Cybersecurity Report" By CISCO
https://www.cisco.com/c/en/us/products/security/security-reports.html

"Cyber Risks Report 2017" by FireEye
https://www.fireeye.com/content/dam/fireeye-www/global/en/current-threats/pdfs/rpt-world-eco-forum.pdf

"M-Trends 2018" by Mandiant FireEye
https://www.fireeye.com/content/dam/collateral/en/mtrends-2018.pdf

"The Cyber Threat to UK Business, 2017-2018 Report," by The GCHQ National Cyber Security Center, UK
http://www.nationalcrimeagency.gov.uk/publications/890-the-cyber-threat-to-uk-business-2017-2018/file

Made in the USA
Columbia, SC
20 September 2021